Collins  ramblers

The Lake District

guide to 30 of the best walking routes

John Gillham and Ronald Turnbull

Collins ® is a registered trademark of HarperCollins Publishers Limited

The authors assert their moral right to be identified as the authors of this work. All rights reserved.

Series Editor Richard Sale
© in this edition HarperCollins Publishers
© in the text John Gillham and Ronald Turnbull
© all photographs John Gillham and Ronald Turnbull with the exception of the following images:
page 6 Skylark © Rob Christiaans/Shutterstock images
page 7 Red Squirrel © Dean Mitchell/Shutterstock images

Mapping on the inner front cover generated from Collins Bartholomew digital databases.

This product uses map data licensed from Ordnance Survey ® with
the permission of the Controller of Her Majesty's Stationery Office.
© Crown copyright. Licence number 399302

The authors would like to thank Chris Chinn (Wallowbarrow), Thomas Turnbull (Borrowdale) and
Peter Wilde of the Mountain Ringlet Survey. Thanks as always to the rangers and path workers of
the LDNP and the National Trust.

We are grateful to the following members of the Ramblers' Association who kindly assisted in
checking the walks in this book: Bill Askew, Paul Atkins, Elizabeth Barraclough, S Benson,
Wendy J A Bowen, A G Brooks, J A C Chodzko, Liz Crocombe, Alan Duval, Elizabeth Fell,
Eric G Fleet, Margaret Gibson, Les Halliman, JF Haysom, Graham D Hole, Philip & Eileen
Holland, B K Jones, Peter Jones, M J Leverton, John Lightfoot, C K Mills, J R Peat, A Prentice,
A & S Reynolds, Bob Scanlan, Peter B Vollands and Sheila Watson.

Printed in China by South China Printing Co. Ltd.   ISBN 978 0 00 738991 9

email: roadcheck@harpercollins.co.uk
Twitter.com/CollinsMaps

Contents

Introduction

The idea of a National Park was conceived in Lakeland – William Wordsworth thought of it in 1821 – and Lakeland remains the ideal and archetype of the National Park. A National Park should not be confused with a National Desert, or a National Wilderness. A park is a created place, a place where the wild and the civilised are tangled up together making somewhere better than either.

Stand on Seathwaite Fell, and look southwest towards Sty Head. The little stone causeway of the National Trust Path Team lies on the foundations of an old packway. It runs between grey crags, on which even individual cracks and handholds have been given names, and over lumpy grassland whose apparent wildness is down to the charcoal-burners and before them the tree-clearers of the Bronze Age. Then look the other way into Borrowdale, at the patterned stone walls and white-sided farmhouses, and even the multicoloured glitter of a car park.

It is this unique combination of crag and café – of ice-climb and ice cream shop – or of the slippery gill and the hollyhocks of the cottage garden, that makes Lakeland the place it is for a walk on the wild (but at the same time civilised) side.

Wasdale, from above Sty Head

Limited as we are by the confines of one book, we have tried to put in something of everything. There are rough rocky climbs and mountain paths. There's a limestone walk. There are walks in the woods, and walks around the lake. We suppose our standard reader to go in for a standard hill walk, taking six or seven hours and crossing a couple of the higher mountains before descending to a pint of Jennings Sneck Lifter and a Cumberland sausage. However, the standard reader is a human being and therefore unpredictable. Sometimes she (or he) feels inspired to try something longer and more demanding among the precipices of Scafell. Sometimes it really is too nasty for the heights, and he (or she) prefers a long but level wander along the valley floor. There may be children along, or only an evening free, so some walks are short in miles while remaining long in views, crags and unexpected footbridges.

We couldn't take you everywhere we wanted in a mere thirty walks. Depending on your definition, the number of lakes and mountains can vary. For the purposes of this book, however,

Lakeland has eight lakes; we'll go halfway round just two of them. We'll walk the floors of Eskdale and Borrowdale – but Lakeland has eleven valleys. We'll climb just 67 of the mountains, and look wistfully through blue air at the other 248. We'll do just a couple of the easier scrambles, and ignore the whole sport of the slimy waterfall, the loose and untrodden crag.

This book may start you on a lifetime of Lakeland summits. We hope it will also introduce you to the Lakeland of valleys, lakesides, woods and waterfalls.

Natural History of Lakeland

Stony Heights

For the last ten thousand years the world has been warming up. Post-glacial plant life that once covered England has been retreating northwards and upwards. The heights of Lakeland are 'Arctic-Alpine': they have more in common with Iceland or Zermatt than with the rest of Cumbria.

Lichen on pink porphyry, Hollin How above Wallowbarrow Gorge

The stony plateaux of the central fells form Lakeland's most distinctive habitat. It is not a very productive one – for an obvious reason. No soil, so no plants.

Or at least, very few plants. Even excluding orange peel, naturalists have spotted around the cairn on Scafell Pike five flowering plants, six mosses and twenty species of lichen. Woolly hair moss is the one that forms grey lumps, rather like dry dead tufts of grass.

Lichens cannot tolerate pollution. Lakeland has little industry and a constant supply of clean air from the west, and lichens flourish here. *Lecidea dicksonii* is the rusty-red one, common on the boulders of Broad Crag but lacking a common English name. The bright yellow-green map lichen resembles the maps of Harveys rather than Ordnance Survey. Dog lichen is the grey crinkly one.

For life forms less robust than lichen, conditions are harsh – lying snow, hard frosts, heavy grazing by sheep, and trampling by human beings. Wind snatches moisture from the leaves; rain washes goodness from the soil. Nevertheless, here as elsewhere, nature has found a way. At certain points among the rock faces (especially in the chemically rich Borrowdale Volcanic), water flushes minerals back out from underground. Here, on high ledges or the walls of gills, grow real rock gardens, with such

Roseroot and Alpine lady's mantle mark a mineral-rich seepage high on Helvellyn

Alpine species as saxifrage, stonecrop, Alpine lady's mantle and Alpine saw-wort. Rarer are the shrubby rock-rose (*Potentilla fruticosa*) of Pillar and Wastwater Screes; the mountain avens; and, in a single gill on Grasmoor, the alpine catchfly. Diminished upland versions of commoner plants can be found too: red campion, wood anemone, and thrift.

It is interesting to note the different ways these plants have evolved to deal with the drying-out effect. Some store water: either in succulent leaves (the stonecrops), or with a bulky root system (moss campion). Others keep down low out of the wind: for example, the least willow, a true tree that reaches maturity at only 1 inch (30mm) high near the summit of Helvellyn.

High Lakeland has been described (by J.A.G. Barnes) as an 'ornithological desert'. There's not much bird-food up here. However, various species use the crags for nest sites: peregrine falcon, buzzard, and kestrel; carrion crow, jackdaw and raven; and Mardale's famous golden eagle. A spectacular sight on hot afternoons is a flock of swifts. They sieve the air for insects in jerky swooping flight above the very summits – close enough overhead that you can hear the wind in their feathers.

Grassy uplands
A more familiar sort of terrain, seen also in the Pennines for example, is the high-level coarse grassland of the eastern fells. The soil is thin, peaty and acid. Even so, in late Spring you can find tiny but bright wildflowers down among the grasses: tormentil and heath bedstraw the most obvious, with lousewort, milkwort and eyebright. Where lime-rich ground-water seeps out, there grow spotted orchids and the delicate silver-white grass of Parnassus.

Skylark

Boggy bits support asphodel, bogbean, bog myrtle, and the colourful sphagnum mosses. Cotton grass has unjointed stems, so is in fact a sedge; reindeer moss is actually a lichen. The carnivorous plants sundew and butterwort snatch their minerals out of the air by trapping flying insects, while bladderwort catches insects floating in sluggish streams. Lakeland has twenty-two species of butterfly and moth.

We see few of the larger ground nesting birds – the curlew, oystercatcher and lapwing who are so noisy in Spring above the Pennines and Southern Uplands. Perhaps in Lakeland they are discouraged by walkers and our dogs. However, skylarks sing at 2,600ft (800m) above High Street and the

Dodds, with the plover, pipit, and wheatear. Red grouse live in Lakeland's patches of heather upland: Back o' Skiddaw, and over the dull country between Borrowdale and Thirlmere.

Woods
All of the valleys and lower slopes up to 1,600ft (500m) were originally woodland: oak on drier ground, birch and alder on wetter. Most of this has been cut down by man, with sheep nibbling to death any attempted re-growth. Some woodland survives, notably in Borrowdale.

Red squirrel

Even those patches that can claim continuity since the Ice Age have been ravaged underneath by sheep. There is little plant life or undergrowth. However, there are glorious mosses and lichens on the ancient tree trunks. Ferns sprout into the dim green light, and fifty different species of fungus have been counted on a single plot of 12 sq. yd (10m²).

Water
Like the hills themselves, the hill tarns and streams are low in nutrients. In the becks, the agile trout can cope with the way the environment keeps flowing rapidly away, and at least what food there is does keep coming past.

In valley tarns and lakes there's a richer bottom sludge, supporting pike, perch, water bugs and beetles, frogs and toads. Char thrive in the larger lakes. Dragonflies appreciate unpolluted air and water; Lakeland has many species. Waterside birds include common sandpiper, heron and dipper. The whooper swan is a distinguished winter visitor.

Animals
Lakeland's wild animals have learnt to keep away from the crowds. The average walker probably won't see any of the resident mammals apart from rabbits. Your best chance is to walk soon after sunrise, or else late into a long summer evening. Hare and fox can be seen in grassy areas, while the woods shelter red squirrel, badger, roe and other introduced deer.

The commonest mammal is the lowly field vole. He isn't a mouse – the mouse is rounded, with a long tail, while the vole is oval, with a stump of tail only. In winter he tunnels between grass and snow, and where snow has just melted you may spot the resulting half-tunnels. The vole converts rough grass into tasty living food for buzzard, kestrel, owl, fox, stoat, weasel, pine marten and adder.

We have given each walk a grade. Note that this grade assesses only the difficulty of a walk. A walk may be short but serious (e.g. Haystacks) or long but otherwise easy (e.g. Ullswater). Along with this grading, consider also the estimated time and maximum altitude.

GRADE 5
A rugged high-level mountain walk involving scrambling. While all scrambling requires care (and become much more serious in wind or Winter), the scrambles in this book are of scrambling Grade 1 and a rope would not normally be used. Ability to navigate with a compass is required.

GRADE 4
A rugged high-level mountain walk. In mist, ability to navigate with compass or GPS required. An OS or Harveys map with full contour detail should be carried in case of straying from the routes. In winter conditions, a Grade 4 or 5 will become a serious expedition calling for ice axe and possibly crampons and should be attempted by experienced walkers only.

Walking conditions and weather

During the summer months, Lakeland weather is never so bad that a well-equipped walker can't head up to the summits, and even enjoy being there. However, it is very changeable. In 2010, accidents involving hypothermia (exposure) occurred not only in winter but in May, July and September.

Walking outside the main season can be very rewarding. When there is snow on the fells, walks graded 4 and 5 become serious and interesting expeditions, usually requiring the ice axe. They should then be attempted only by those with appropriate skills and equipment.

The central fells are rough and rocky. Progress can be surprisingly slow. Paths are many and confusing, and there are crags around. If mist descends, those without maps and compasses can get into trouble. The hills are busy, and on summer weekends someone will always come along. Most are happy to help the navigationally challenged if asked. Bear in mind that those with the newest and most expensive jackets aren't necessarily the best map readers, and that few are honest enough to confess 'sorry mate, I'm lost myself'.

With each walk we indicate the maximum altitude. This is not only to emphasise the difficulty of any peaks involved, but also to show the seriousness of the expedition. Anywhere above 1,500ft (400m) or so must be considered hill country. Above 2,000ft (600m) the weather will be a layer-of-clothing nastier than it is at the car park, and could quite quickly turn much nastier than that.

Maps, waymarking and access

Although it may be possible to follow your chosen route using the map and description in this book together with a compass, we strongly recommend that a map with full contour detail – Ordnance Survey or Harveys – be carried.

The Ordnance Survey's 1:50,000 Landrangers are satisfactory for straight-forward routes on marked paths and ridges. Sheets 89, 90, 96 and 97 cover the Lake District.

For field paths, or fell walking off the beaten track, you need a larger scale map. The sheets OL4, OL5, OL6 and OL7 of the Ordnance Survey Explorer series are at 1:25,000. They mark field boundaries even in the low country. They are doublesided, showing much interesting ground around the main fells at no extra cost.

The Harveys Superwalker maps at 1:25,000 have excellent contour detail and mark walls and fences on the hill. There are six sheets (Lakeland North, East, West and Central, South-East and South-West). The maps are waterproof.

Public rights of way in the cultivated valley bottoms (coloured yellow on Harveys maps) are almost always waymarked with all necessary stiles and signposts. Paths on the open fell are not waymarked. Some are marked with cairns, but these are usually either too few or too many to be helpful.

In those cultivated valley bottoms walkers should remain on public rights of way. There is a general presumption of access anywhere on the open fell, which in 'Access Areas' marked on Explorer maps is a legal right.

Crowd management
Lakeland has the best walking in England – some would say, in the world. So it is very popular. If you prefer some measure of solitude, then walk outside the holiday months of July and August (which are, scenically speaking, two of the less rewarding months anyway). Walk on weekdays. Walk in bad weather. During long summer days, start early (few leave the car park before 10.00am) or stay out late (on cloudless evenings in June it gets dark at around 10.30pm).

Looking after Lakeland
Most walkers will be familiar with the Country Code. Apart from points already mentioned, this asks you to fasten all gates (unless they were fastened open already), to keep dogs under control (in sight always, and on a lead when passing livestock), to leave no litter, and to cross fences and walls at gates or stiles. Please don't park so as to obstruct gateways or passing places.

Walkers' cars do more damage than walkers ever do. Every time you manage to get to a walk by public transport you make public transport more viable and help towards the eventual elimination of the car.

Microbial infections such as Giardia are not yet a problem in Lakeland. To keep it that way, do not pee near streams, and bury solid wastes. To make things slightly less nasty for your fellow-walkers, please use sphagnum moss rather than toilet paper, but if you use toilet paper bury that too or take it away in a plastic bag.

GRADE 3
A moderately demanding walk. Either a mountain walk on grassy ridges and paths, or a lower one involving steep slopes or rough ground and possibly some navigational ability.

GRADE 2
A fairly straightforward walk, below the 2,000ft (600m) contour. Some stretches may be off paths, and field paths may require some navigation skills (e.g. head NW to find the next stile).

GRADE 1
A low-level walk on clear paths with no particularly steep or rough sections.

Cat Bells, Derwentwater and Blencathra

Fact file

Tourist information
Ambleside ☎ 015394 32582
Bowness ☎ 015394 42895
Coniston ☎ 015394 41533
Glenridding ☎ 017684 82414
Grange-over-Sands ☎ 015395 34026
Keswick ☎ 017687 72645
Pooley Bridge ☎ 017684 86135
www.cumbria-the-lake-district.co.uk
www.visitcumbria.com

Transport (road, rail, water)
Lakeland is surrounded by railway lines, and has a usable bus network into most of the valleys. There is a free timetable and a transport phone number.
Rail info: ☎ 08457 48 49 50   www.nationalrail.co.uk
Cumbria travel line (bus and train): ☎ 0871 200 2233
Lakes Rider timetable: free from any Tourist Information Office or Stagecoach bus
Internet journey planner: www.travelinenortheast.info
Ullswater Steamers:
☎ 017684 82229   www.ullswater-steamers.co.uk
Derwentwater Launch:
☎ 017687 72263   www.keswick-launch.co.uk
Ravenglass & Eskdale Railway timetable info:
☎ 01229 717171   www.ravenglass-railway.co.uk

Historic inns, B&Bs and youth hostels are plentiful and many are inexpensive. YHA info and bookings www.yha.org.uk. There are campsites, and the network of camping barns offers basic shelter for about £6 a night. Camping Barn info and bookings at Keswick Tourist Information.

Weather and other
National Park weatherline (one-day, with fell top conditions in winter) ☎ 0844 846 2444
www.metoffice.gov.uk/loutdoor/mountainsafety/
(with felltop conditions in winter)
www.mwis.org.uk/ld.php (3-day mountain forecast)
Harvey Maps:
☎ 01786 841202   www.harveymaps.co.uk
Ordnance Survey maps:
www.ordnancesurvey.co.uk/mapshop

How to use this book

This book contains route maps and descriptions for 30 walks. Each walk is graded and areas of interest are indicated by symbols (see below). For each walk particular points of interest are denoted by a number both in the text and on the map (where the number appears in a circle). In the text the route instructions are prefixed by a capital letter. We recommend that you read the whole description, including the tinted box at the start of each walk, before setting out.

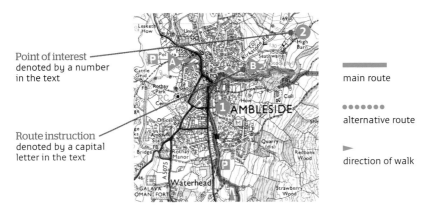

Point of interest
denoted by a number
in the text

Route instruction
denoted by a capital
letter in the text

━━━━━
main route

●●●●●●●●
alternative route

▶
direction of walk

Key to walk symbols

The walks in this book are graded from 1–5 according to the level of difficulty, with 1 (green) being the easiest and 5 (red) the most difficult. We recommend that walks graded 4 or higher (or grade 3 (amber) where indicated) should only be undertaken by experienced walkers who are competent in the use of map and compass and who are aware of the difficulties of the terrain they will encounter. The use of detailed maps is recommended for all routes.

At the start of each walk there is a series of symbols that indicate particular areas of interest associated with the route.

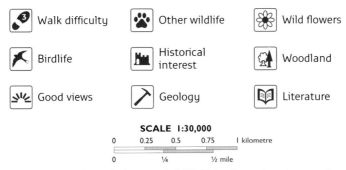

Walk difficulty

Other wildlife

Wild flowers

Birdlife

Historical interest

Woodland

Good views

Geology

Literature

SCALE 1:30,000

0   0.25   0.5   0.75   I kilometre

0   ¼   ½ mile

Please note the scale for maps is 1:30,000 unless otherwise stated
North is always at the top of the page

The Langdale Pikes

START/FINISH:
Car park at Elterwater
Common (NY329051)

DISTANCE/ASCENT:
13 miles (21km) / 3,300ft
(1,000m)

APPROXIMATE TIME:
8½ hours

HIGHEST POINT:
Harrison Stickle 2,415ft (736m)

MAP:
OS Explorer OL6 and OL7;
OS Landranger 90;
Harveys Lakeland Central

REFRESHMENTS:
Old Dungeon Ghyll Hotel,
Great Langdale;
The Britannia, Elterwater;
the Wainwright Inn,
Chapel Stile

ADVICE:
Routes from Elterwater
Common across Blea Rigg to
Stickle Tarn are complex and
can be very confusing in mist

The Langdale Pikes are the peacocks of Lakeland, receiving admiring gazes from the tourists in the car parks of Dungeon Ghyll and on the shores of Windermere. From here their near-vertical flanks of rock can be seen rising boastfully into the clouds.

This long approach from Elterwater Lakes takes in the side the tourist cameras don't reach and seeks a wider perspective of the Langdales – you'll see a long knobbly ridge, a fine cliff face, the tame grassy western flanks, and an ancient industrial site.

❶ Elterwater NY327047

Elterwater sits by the gates of Great Langdale, where Yew Crag and Dow Bank have squeezed the valley pastures into a narrow sliver of green, north of its small glacial lake. The situation seems very peaceful and pastoral, but occasionally the peace is shattered by thunderous explosions from the nearby slate quarries. The green slate quarried here is much sought after, and has been used in famous buildings all over the world, including the Old Bailey in London, St Paul's Tower in Dallas, and the Connaught Centre in Hong Kong.

A▶ Turn right out of the car park to climb on the winding High Close road. Just after a left-hand bend take a short-cut path on the right through bracken and thistle to reach the road a little higher up and just above the junction with the upper Chapel Stile lane.

Immediately across the road, follow a small path climbing northeast up slopes of bracken. The path steepens and becomes stony, climbing past a small stone enclosure hiding an electricity substation. It rises below Huntingstile Crag to a pass where the descending path ahead would lead down towards Grasmere.

B▶ At the top point of the pass, turn left on a smaller path that climbs among small crags and holly. It weaves its way up Dow Bank and Spedding Crag. To the right you will see Silver Howe with its reddish scree gully; to the left there is a view down to Elterwater's slate quarry.

Head northwest on an undulating course over rocky bluffs and marshy depressions. Sometimes the path is good, but occasionally it disappears for a short distance into the moor grasses. The main thing is to keep roughly northwest up the broad and bumpy crest, which becomes more rocky as you gain height.

Harrison Stickle, Pavey Ark and Stickle Tarn from Blea Rigg

After a roughly level section, the path forks. The right fork takes in the side-hump of Silver Howe, so take the left fork, which crosses the top of the left-hand flank before regaining the bumpy crest beyond. Now the view is along the gently curving fields of Great Langdale and heathery Lingmoor Fell, which is overtopped by the rugged Coniston fells.

C▶ After 2 miles (3km) from the beginning of the ridge, the path comes upon a rushy pool, with Lang How behind. If it is calm the pools give a reflection of the distinctive summits of the Langdale Pikes. The devious path twists and turns to the right of the tarns and, after a further ¾ mile (1km), makes a detour to the Easedale side of the ridge at Great Castle How. Beyond this knoll it visits some more pools, threading between two on the left and one on the right.

The ground ahead now swells to Blea Rigg and the path keeps to the right of some marshy ground, passing to the

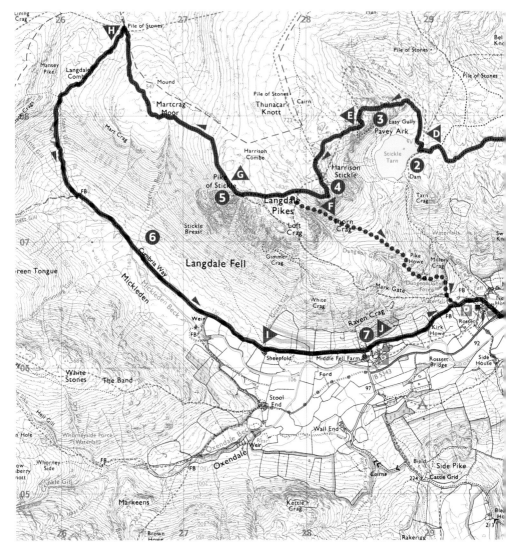

south of the summit cairn. Easedale Tarn has come into view down on your right.

The ridge levels off, with a couple of peat hags. Now the main ridge rises to the rocky peak of Sergeant Man, but our route bears slightly left (west), gently downhill, towards the impressive crag of Pavey Ark. Very soon Stickle Tarn comes into view ahead and slightly below. Descend to the northeastern shore of the lake. It is not easy to locate this path, especially in hill fog.

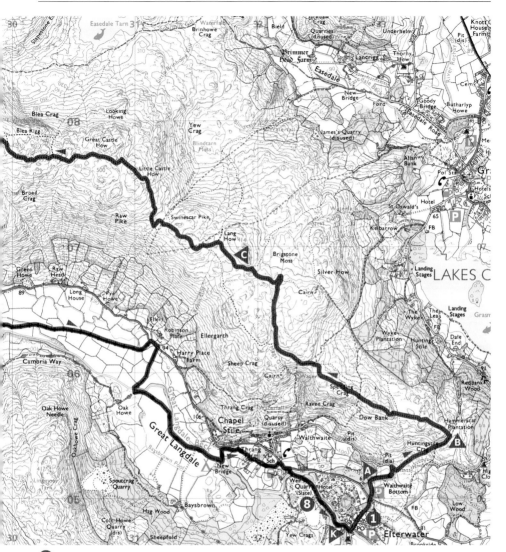

② Stickle Tarn NY287077

Pavey Ark dominates the scene hereabouts, rearing up from Stickle Tarn in impressive splintered cliffs. The ledge that cuts diagonally left across the cliffs is Jack's Rake, a popular route for scramblers; the gully starting at the same place but cutting up right is Easy Gully, an entertaining but simple scramble with difficult boulders to negotiate near the top.

The dam was built across Stickle Tarn, not to make it into a drinking water reservoir, but to regulate the supply of water

Looking over Great Langdale from Harrison Stickle

to the gunpowder works in Elterwater. The works sent an employee every Monday to open the sluice gates and every Friday to close them again.

D▶ Turn right and follow the path climbing alongside the eastern bank of Bright Beck. In 330yds (300m) the path divides (NY289081). The path continuing along the bank heads for High Raise. Leave this for the much wider one crossing the beck and climbing grassy slopes, aiming right of Pavey Ark's cliffs. The route, named by Wainwright as North Rake, goes up a stony spur, with many large cairns. Halfway up, a short detour path to the left takes you to the top of Easy Gully, from where there is a spectacular view down to Stickle Tarn. The path continues up an open gully, with a low crag rising on its left.

Pavey Ark's summit, a rocky outcrop, lies beyond a derelict wall on the left.

❸ Pavey Ark NY285079
Technically speaking, Pavey Ark isn't a true summit: it's just an outlying crag of Thunacar Knott. Purists can head west for the little cairn of this grassy summit. Most walkers, however, will be happy to make Harrison Stickle their next peak, and it's a simple plod to get there.

E▶ After descending southwest to join the Thunacar Knott path by a small pool, the path climbs south to the summit cairn of Harrison Stickle.

❹ Harrison Stickle NY282074
Harrison Stickle looks very impressive from Langdale; a towering pike that has been likened to a lion's head. Langdale

looks equally good from Harrison Stickle, its lush green fields dividing the rocky sides of Blea Rigg and Lingmoor Fell from the plains around Windermere.

F An eroded stony path descends west towards Pike of Stickle, a bell-like dome of rock when seen from hereabouts. The path dips into the peaty hollow that is the head of Dungeon Ghyll (the stream). A path to the left, which descends above and left of the stream, is an escape and shortcut to New Dungeon Ghyll (the hotel). Meanwhile the main path ahead crosses the peaty hollow that is the head of Dungeon Ghyll, then climbs across grassy slopes to the foot of the peak. You then turn left to scramble up the rocks to Pike of Stickle's summit.

5 Pike of Stickle NY273073

And what a summit Pike of Stickle is! You can now see that the bell described earlier has grown in stature to become a domed cathedral of volcanic rock towering above the bare valley of Mickleden. To the southeast you look across to one of Lakeland's great climbing crags – that of Gimmer.

Gimmer Crag above
Great Langdale

G Retrace your route of ascent to the foot of the crags, then follow the little path northwest for 1¼ mile (2km) down Martcrag Moor towards the small tarn at Stake Pass – notice the glacial moraines deposited here after the last ice age.

H Just before the tarn, a well-used path descends left (southwest) into Langdale Combe, crosses Stake Gill then zigzags down steep slopes beneath Black Crags. It joins the Rossett Gill path at a wooden footbridge over Mickleden Beck. Now at the valley bottom you trace the wide track alongside the northern bank of the beck and beneath the lower scree slopes of Pike of Stickle.

⑥ Axe Factory NY270070

High on those scree slopes Neolithic men discovered a bed of greenish, flinty volcanic tuff amid the thick layers of Borrowdale Volcanics. The grey-green rock was ideal for the manufacture of stone axes and implements, as it could be given a sharp edge.

Chipping sites have been found on Martcrag Moor and Harrison Stickle, and some historians believe that a man-made cave high in the scree gully east of Pike of Stickle was a shelter for several factory workers. Axes from the Langdale factory were hewn into a rough shape and sent to the Cumbrian coast for polishing by sandstone. They would then have been carried by ship to other settlements in Britain.

▶ As the track turns the corner into Great Langdale, the valley floor widens and the rough grasslands of Mickleden are transformed into greener farm pastures.

Before the first buildings the track divides. The lower gate leads to the Old Dungeon Ghyll Hotel, but the route continues through the upper one and above Middle Fell Farm.

⑦ Old Dungeon Ghyll Hotel NY286061

This famous old inn, once known as the Middlefell Inn, has long been a favourite with both climbers and walkers. It is the Lakeland equivalent of Wales' Pen y Gwryd. One of the more famous visitors to the inn was the Emperor of Japan, who came to climb here in 1915. Other visitors include Himalayan climbers Don Whillans, Joe Brown, Lord Hunt, Charles Evans and Tom Bourdillon.

▶ After passing behind (if you're that disciplined) the Old Dungeon Ghyll Hotel, follow the enclosed path eastwards beneath Raven Crag. The path joins the path down from Stickle Tarn and turns right past the New Dungeon Ghyll Hotel and Sticklebarn Tavern to the road.

Now take a walled gravel track, which begins in the car park across the road, and heads east by Great Langdale Beck at first, then across fields to its north. After a mile the track rejoins the road.

Turn right along the road for 90yds (80m), then right again onto a track aiming south to cross the beck via a footbridge. Turn left on a new track, traversing fields close to the riverbank, and passing a camp site. It wiggles left to recross

the beck at another bridge, then right beside quarry waste and behind some cottages on the outskirts of Chapel Stile. Where the track turns left to rejoin the road, leave it for a path going straight on, past Thrang Farm. Cross a triangle of grass onto another walled path, out onto the road by the Wainwright Inn. A man mending a wagon wheel on the inn sign shows that this has nothing to do with Alfred Wainwright.

Great Langdale from Spedding Crag

After following the road past the inn, turn right through a gate, then left to cross the footbridge over the beck. A path to the left continues by the wooded beckside and beneath the slate piles of old quarry workings.

8 The Elterwater Gunpowder Works NY327051
On the other side of the beck there used to be a gunpowder works. Between 1824 and 1929, when it closed, there were six active water wheels powering twelve mills where the powder was ground. At its peak, around eighty locals, who were referred to as powder monkeys, were employed at the works. After its closure, most of the buildings were burned and demolished to remove the possibility of any remaining gunpowder causing accidents, but some were allowed to stand. These are now used by the Langdale Time Share.

▶ The path joins a tarmac lane (the access road to the huge quarry on the hillsides above) and meets a back road from Little Langdale, close to Elterwater Youth Hostel. Turn left, go over the bridge, then keep straight on to pass the Britannia Inn and the village green back to the car park.

Bowfell

START/FINISH:
Old Dungeon Ghyll Hotel
(NY286060), where parking is
limited; or New Dungeon Ghyll
with Langdale car park opposite
the hotel and National Trust's
Stickle Gill car park 200m later
(NY296064)

DISTANCE/ASCENT:
10 miles (16km) from the Old
Dungeon and 12 miles (19km)
from the New Dungeon /
3,600ft (1,100m)

APPROXIMATE TIME:
8 or 9 hours

HIGHEST POINT:
Bowfell summit 2,963ft (903m)

MAP:
OS Explorer OL6;
OS Landranger 89 or 90;
Harveys Lakeland Central

REFRESHMENTS:
Stickle Barn Tavern,
Great Langdale

ADVICE:
The rock-step on the Crinkle
Crags can be avoided, but the
Crinkles themselves are very
tricky in mist. The only safe
escape from this route back to
Langdale is from Three Tarns by
way of the Band or Buscoe Syke

At the head of Langdale are two fine mountains – or
seven, depending on how many Crinkle Crags you think
there are. The crossing of the Crinkles and Bowfell is high
stony hill walking of the most serious sort. In addition,
there are two even more interesting moments. The 'Bad
Step' on Long Top is a short overhanging rock climb;
the slender can avoid it by passing through a hole,
anyone else by taking a side-path. On the other hand,
the scramble onto Bowfell is gentle and pleasant, with
a large path alongside. A short diversion allows the eye
to slide down a fascinating geological feature: Bowfell's
Great Slab.

1 Langdale NY294065
In the bottom of Langdale are two historic inns. The more
convenient car park for this walk is at the Old Dungeon Ghyll.
Our route description starts at the larger car parks at the
New Dungeon Ghyll, as they are more likely to have spaces.
But start at the Old Hotel if you can.

A Just past the Langdale car park, and opposite the
National Trust's Stickle Gill one, a farm track signed for Oak
Howe leaves the tarred road. Go to left of the farm, cross a
footbridge, and turn up to a ladder stile on the right, which
starts a permissive path along the valley side. After almost
²/₃ mile (1km) it passes along above a wood. At the end of

The celebrated 'Bad Step' on Long Top of the Crinkle Crags

On the Crinkle Crags

the wood turn down through a gate (stile alongside) and a kissing gate on the left into the National Trust camp site. Turn left to follow a track right through the camp site, to turn right on the road descending from Blea Tarn.

The road crosses the valley floor towards the Old Hotel, but where it bends sharply right, turn off left on the track to Stool End Farm.

At the end of the farmyard, follow the track by the wall on your left, ignoring the tracks on the right to Mickleden and the Band, and go through a gate. A footbridge crosses Oxendale Beck and starts the large path leading up towards Red Tarn in the gap between Pike of Blisco and Cold Pike.

The path runs up beside the small gorge of Browney Gill. Just past the top of the gorge, and just before the tarn, you reach a cross-path. Here turn up right, ascending gradually between Cold Pike on the left and Great Knott on the right. The path curves round onto a peak usually referred to as the first Crinkle 2,736ft (834m).

② The First Crinkle NY250046
The view east is down the rocky slope to Langdale, now a satisfying 2,000ft (600m) below. The slate farmhouses date from the seventeenth and eighteenth centuries but the field

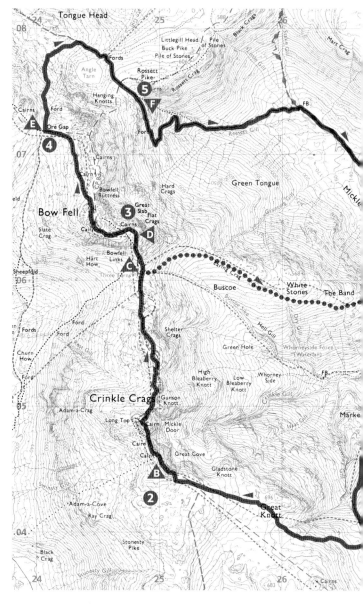

pattern is much older; the wall surrounding the valley head is thirteenth-century. Southward is a flat moor with many pools with the Coniston tops peeping over the rim. The contrasting views allow a moment of landscape philosophy. The bleak and the pretty are in alliance. Lakeland's special quality is to be Civilisation and Wilderness, mixed.

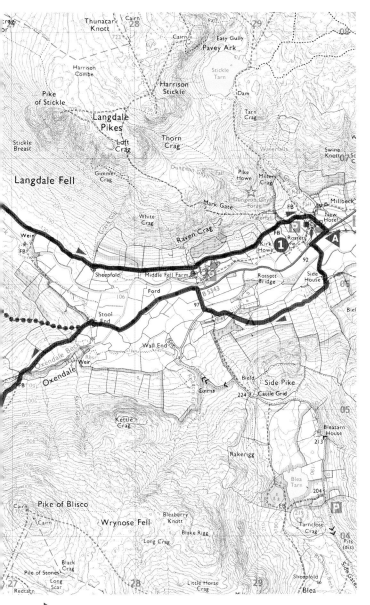

B A stony clamber, with sudden drops to Langdale on the right, leads to the col before Long Top – that being the second and highest of several tops that make up the Crinkle Crags.

The path up Long Top ascends a shallow gully to a cave. Now good, well-scratched holds lead up the overhanging wall on

Three Tarns, view to Mickledore

the right. There is also, for dogs, children and the slim, a route up through a hole at the back of the cave; you won't get your rucksack through without a person at the top to lift it out. If you don't like the overhang or the hole, then contour to the left from the gully foot for 120yds (110m). A path now leads up onto Long Top.

Thread your way through the various rocky tops of the Crinkles. Even though there is a path, the ground is complex and confusing in mist. In these circumstances, no route description can help you. Just head north by the compass. Where the compass points over a hummock, don't try to walk round the side of it. Doing this in mist tends to find you down in Mosedale. The end of the Crinkle Crags is the col of the Three Tarns.

The path down to the right here is a short-cut or escape route back to Langdale. From the Three Tarns the main route continues on a broad stony path ascending directly up the face of Bowfell. This could be taken, but it is much more pleasant to scramble on the easy-angled, clean rocks immediately to the right of the path. The path reaches flatter ground at a col; the scramble arrives on a 15ft (5m) knoll just to the east.

From the knoll, continue northwards for 55yds (50m) to reach the top of steep ground. Turn left, heading northwest along the top of the steep ground for about 2 minutes to find the top edge of the Great Slab. Note that it is not necessary to descend into the steep rocky ground on the right to find the Slab.

③ Great Slab NY246065
The view outward is a fine one, but it is also worth looking down at the slab underfoot. Near the top its surface bears ripple-marks left by water long ago. We are looking down on a fossilised lake bed which is five hundred million years old. Geologists know it was a lake bed, and not the sea floor, because in the age called the Ordovician the sea was full of life whereas the land was not; Great Slab has no fossils in it. The rock of the slab is a tuff, a sedimentary rock formed by ash from the surrounding volcanoes settling on the lake floor. Confident scramblers can walk around on the slab itself, provided the rock is dry, but be aware that the rock is rather mossy and that a fall here could be very serious indeed.

On the summit of Bowfell

D▶ The top of the Great Slab is just below the well-used path from Three Tarns to Bowfell. This path crosses the shoulder of Bowfell with the summit on the left.

From the summit descend north to rejoin the cairned path, which winds down to a col. It then follows easier ground on the left (western) flank, to Ore Gap.

❹ Ore Gap NY241072
Iron ore is found in the rocks here, and iron rust stains the water that trickles out of the col.

E▶ At Ore Gap turn down right on the rebuilt path to Angle Tarn. The path crosses the outflow on stepping stones and climbs to a col. At your toes now is Rossett Gill. This gully is a steep and troublesome descent over rocks and loose stones.

❺ Rossett Gill NY247075
If you make the short climb to Rossett Pike, just up on the left, you'll get a good view of the Great Slab, and see how its bedding is copied in the surrounding crags.

There are two tricks to ease the tough descent of Rossett Gill that follows. The first is to be a geologist. The gully walls show particularly clearly and interestingly the different types

Great Slab, Bowfell

of tuffs (compacted volcanic ash, remember) and lava flows. The gully is part of a fault line that continues across the head of Langdale to Blea Tarn; it was the line of weakness that steered the glacier along Mickleden. In the other direction, the fault helped define the steep faces of Great End and Gable. As the two bodies of rock moved past each other, they shattered each other at the point of contact. Such fault line shattering is evident in the gully walls, and in the rubble that forms its floor.

The second, and easier trick for Rossett Gill, though, is not to go down the gully at all. A pony track leaves it on the right.

▶ Unless keen on geology, then, descend only the first 100ft (30m) (vertical) of Rossett Gill, and as the gully walls rise, find the cairned path leading out to the right. This path, which was built for ponies, zigzags down the steep rocky slopes to right of the gully.

A broad track leads along the floor of Mickleden, to arrive just above the Old Dungeon Ghyll. If for some reason you don't wish to drop into this welcoming pub, continue ahead through the upper gate along a stony walled track that rises slightly, then drops to cross the Dungeon Ghyll stream before arriving at the New Dungeon Ghyll Hotel.

3 Easedale Round

START/FINISH:
Car park at Grasmere
(NY336073)

DISTANCE/ASCENT:
8½ miles (14km) / 3,100ft
(950m)

APPROXIMATE TIME:
6½ hours

HIGHEST POINT:
Sergeant Man 2,415ft (736m)

MAP:
OS Explorer OL6 and OL7;
OS Landranger 90,
Harveys Lakeland Central

REFRESHMENTS:
Numerous cafés and inns at
Grasmere

ADVICE:
The paths to Easedale Tarn
and descents from Helm Crag
are all on easy-to-follow,
surfaced paths, but the high
ground, especially between
Sergeant Man and Calf Crag, is
confusing in mist. Unless you
are an experienced fellwalker
with good map and compass
skills, save this route for fine,
settled weather

When one thinks of Easedale and Grasmere, one thinks of the Lakeland poets. And when you walk in Easedale, you will walk in the footsteps of William and Dorothy Wordsworth, Samuel Taylor Coleridge and Robert Southey, and see the waterfalls and majestic crags that inspired them. This route takes in the Sour Milk Gill falls and the 'gloomily sublime' Easedale Tarn before climbing to the craggy summits at the head of the valley. And just when the walk seems to be drawing to a close, there's Helm Crag, the Lion and the Lamb. It's the best summit of the day, and there are rocks to play on.

1 Grasmere NY336073
The Grasmere Sports, first held in 1852, have become one of the Lake District's most popular meetings. The events include fell-racing, Cumberland wrestling and hound trailing.

St Oswald's Church has a fourteenth-century tower and a 400-year-old porch, but its simple attractiveness has been spoiled by drab grey rendering. It is one of a handful of churches to conduct rush-bearing ceremonies, which commemorate the days when old rushes were removed from the church floor and replaced with fresh ones. The colourful procession includes girls from the village wearing crowns of flowers, and boys carrying crosses made from rushes.

Sour Milk Gill Falls, Easedale

Easedale Tarn from Blea Rigg

The graves of Dorothy and William Wordsworth lie in the churchyard beneath the yew trees the poet planted. At 29 years of age Wordsworth, with his sister Dorothy, came to live at Dove Cottage, which lies at Town End, just off the main road. Here he wrote some of his best-known works. The poet is commemorated in the church by a bust created by Woolner.

Across the street from the church is the Rectory, where Wordsworth lived for two sad years during which he buried two of his children.

A From the car park turn right along Stock Lane, passing St Oswald's Church. Turn left up Easedale Road. Just beyond Goody Bridge, a fine, stone-built bridge spanning Easedale Beck, the through road bends right, but here continue up the Easedale Road. Turn left on a signposted bridleway which crosses a stream on a slate footbridge, heads west through oak woods, then traverses water meadows, lush with marsh marigolds and milkmaids.

Walkers rounding Sergeant Man

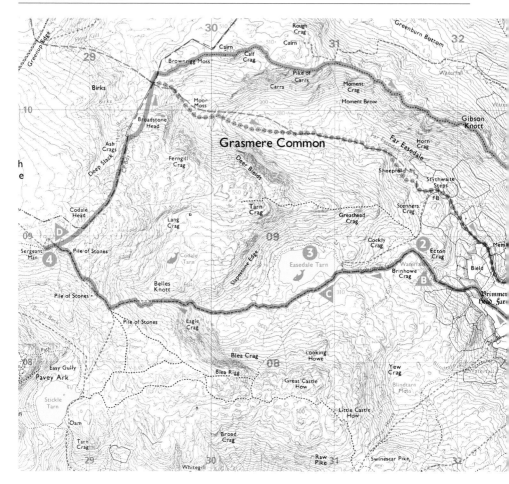

The engineered bridleway steals into Easedale on the south side of the beck. On the right you can see a recently reconstructed packhorse bridge; ahead are the craggy hillsides down which Sour Milk Gill tumbles.

❷ Sour Milk Falls NY317087
Rowan and beech trees are scattered round the rocky fellsides above the stream. You may see willow warblers and white-throats, who love such woodland and scrub areas. Above the falls the landscape becomes bleaker. The rocky fellsides close in, and a little heather mixes with windswept moor grasses.

B▶ The path climbs to the left of the falls, though a tall dry-stone wall does its best in places to stop you seeing the gushing cascades.

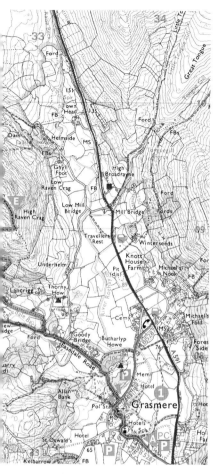

③ Easedale Tarn
NY307087

Easedale Tarn appears – an expansive sheet of water with lilies in it, and echoing with the sound of black-headed gulls. The gulls are used to being fed by humans; if you picnic here, you will have close company. English critic and essayist Thomas de Quincey wrote that Easedale Tarn was the 'most gloomily sublime' of Lakeland tarns. Easedale, in relation to Grasmere, was 'a chapel within a cathedral'.

C The path rounds the tarn on the left (south) side before beginning a climb beneath the sunless Eagle Crag. The stream on the right tumbles down wide, grey slabs, while a perfect pyramidal peak, Belles Knott, captures centre stage in the view ahead, rearing up from the surrounding bracken, ling and rocks. In the upper section of the climb, as you approach Belles Knott, the path crosses some slabs that can be treacherous when wet, and especially when icy.

As the path clambers up between Belles Knott and Eagle Crag it presents you with a choice of routes. The right fork goes to Codale Tarn with a chance to detour to the top of Belles Knott. The left fork, the one to be used on this occasion, maintains its westerly direction, climbing up to the Blea Rigg ridge.

On reaching the brow of the ridge, turn right to follow a path climbing north-west to reach a marshy area filled with a handful of shallow pools. Sergeant Man's rocky summit now lies just a boulder hop away.

Sergeant Man summit

④ Sergeant Man NY286088

From a distance Sergeant Man looks like a knobble on the horizon, but as you draw near, its craggy mountain shape becomes more evident and reasons for climbing it become more compelling. The summit cairn, or 'man', caps a small rocky top surrounded by marshes and some peaty pools. The sergeant may have been an official from Lord Egremont's estate.

D▶ Retrace your steps down the rocks then head in a north-northeast direction across the marshy area, keeping to drier ground to the right of the pools (the course is trackless for a short way). On the rocks of Codale Head a line of iron fence posts highlights the way. A path soon develops and passes several pools that are filled with bogbean. It meets and follows Mere Beck for a while, then comes down to the head of Far Easedale where the bridleway used by Wainwright's *Coast to Coast* cuts across it (NY295103). Following this path down to the right would give a sheltered short cut back to Grasmere.

Go straight across the bridleway, to the far side of the col. Here the path swings right (east) high on the fellsides at the head of Easedale, across Brownrigg Moss and on to Calf Crag. Far Easedale lies spread below on your right, a wild valley with a remote feel belied by its nearness to Grasmere.

The path continues southeast along the ridge past the rocky knoll of Pike of Carrs to Gibson Knott. The path down Gibson Knott is a winding one, threading between rocky outcrops down to a grassy saddle beneath Helm Crag.

Helm Crag, with its curiously-shaped summit rocks, has been beckoning for a while. Now it's just across Bracken Hause, with a stiff climb to get to the summit, but thankfully, a short one too.

The Howitzer, Helm Crag

⑤ Helm Crag NY327094

The first of the summit rock features is known as the Howitzer when seen from Dunmail Raise, or the Old Woman at the Organ when seen from Grasmere. This is a difficult scramble, one that Wainwright regretted not doing. At the further end of the summit ridge are the rocks known as the Lion and the Lamb – they are much easier to scale.

Grasmere village and lake seen from Helm Crag

Helm Crag's east flanks plummet into Rothay Valley from where there is a constant hum of cars speeding up and down the road to Dunmail Raise. Across the green fields of the valley bottom rise the Fairfield and Helvellyn ranges, and you can plot the course of Wainwright's *Coast to Coast* route – a little path climbing the slopes above Tongue Gill.

▶ Beyond the Lion and the Lamb, the path drops to a col and then descends right on grass and rock slopes, with Grasmere's lake and village directly ahead. In the middle reaches of the descent, above White Crag, the path swings right to pass above Jackdaw Crag.

A heavily engineered stone-stepped path then descends by walls into the woodland, passing an old quarry, to reach a little hamlet. Turn left here to reach the Easedale Road, and follow it past Goody Bridge and along the outward route back into Grasmere.

Sometimes even a little fell like Loughrigg Fell can be too much of a toil. Maybe it's too hot, or too windy. Fortunately, Loughrigg has some fine lakes at its foot, and a couple of interesting caves too. So why not walk round Loughrigg, and while you are at it take in Skelwith Force and a cuppa at the Chesters Café, Skelwith Bridge.

① Elterwater NY327047

Set in Great Langdale with the Langdale Pikes as a backdrop, Elterwater village has a picturesque little green, a whitewashed pub, the Britannia Inn and a maple tree with an octagonal seat around it.

From the car park turn right, uphill on the steep, narrow High Close road. At a sharp left-hand bend a path on the right cuts the corner and rejoins the road just above a junction.

Immediately across the road, when you remeet it, a track climbs northeast across slopes of bracken and thistle towards Huntingstile Crag. The public right of way joins in from the right and the path becomes a stony one, climbing beneath the crags past a small stone enclosure hiding an electricity sub-station.

A dry-stone wall comes in from the left as the path reaches a saddle between crags on the left and Hammerscar

Rydal Water from the path round Loughrigg

Plantation. The public right of way heads north by the wall on its way to Grasmere, but the path we want descends into a hollow on the right. It crosses some marshy ground using some stepping stones, then climbs by another wall towards the plantation's left-hand (northern) edge. The path now swings right, descending round a little knoll, and traces the plantation's edge down to the road at Red Bank (NY340057).

Inside Loughrigg Cave

Turn right along the road for about 110yds (100m), then double back left on a wide, stony track through the woods. As you pass through a gate it emerges into the open on Loughrigg Terrace.

2 Loughrigg Terrace NY345058
If you're alone on Loughrigg Terrace, it's either before dawn, after dusk, or the weather is seriously inclement, for this is one of Lakeland's busy places. The path has been heavily engineered, there are little wooden seats all along it, and, worse still, they're all full, meaning you'll have to wait for your picnic. However, the classic view of Grasmere and its village, with Helm Crag, Dunmail Raise and Fairfield rising behind, makes jostling with the crowds worthwhile.

B As Grasmere is left behind, the track swings right, and Rydal Water is about to come into view. Ignore the main bridleway, which descends left to join a wall, and instead traverse the hillsides beneath Ewe Crag. Junipers are now scattered among the bracken and crags. The path comes upon an area of slate spoil, where it joins a quarry track at the entrance to a huge cave on the right.

❸ Loughrigg Cave NY355058
Wainwright jokingly claimed that Loughrigg Cave could house the entire population of Ambleside, although they would have to get their feet wet in its little lake. It's certainly a big cave, blasted by the quarrymen. The Tilberthwaite Tuffs found here were useful as they could easily be split into symmetrical slabs for building.

Elter Water with Langdale Pikes
on the horizon

▶ Descend from the cave entrance on the access track, which zigzags beneath a copse of fine larch trees and another cave – you would have to scramble over some rocks to see this one and it's hardly worth it. Just beyond the crossing of a small stream, turn right onto a faint path that climbs southeast above the woods of Rough Intake.

The path soon establishes itself as a grassy one, forging south-wards through more bracken. It searches out a depression between Loughrigg Fell's summit and two of its outlying rock knolls, and passes an area filled with windwarped juniper.

④ Loughrigg Fell and the Ice Age NY347053
Eighteen thousand years ago, Loughrigg lay beneath the thick ice sheet of the Dunmail Glacier, which also carved out Rydal Water. The ice sheet smoothed and rounded the rocks into the complex formations they are today, while glacial meltwaters hollowed out shallow valleys such as the one you are about to walk through.

▶ There are many paths, so if perplexed just keep south. On reaching higher ground the path hugs the bracken-clad slopes to the left of a marshy grassland channel. Join a wide earth path that arrives from the left, to cross five big stepping stones. Here ignore a small path up to the right (to Loughrigg summit) and pass a tiny tarn. The wide path veers south-southwest with the craggy Park Fell prominent across the Brathay valley.

A wall joins the path, which now swings right, then left. Ignore the descending path through the gate on the left, but stay just above the wall. Beyond a gate the path becomes a stony lane that descends beneath Ivy Crag and past the Tarn Foot camp site.

Elterwater village with Coniston Fells behind

Bear right beyond the lodge at the bottom of the track, on a gravel lane past Dillygate (cottage), then left beyond the terraced cottages down a tarmac lane. This shortly joins the High Close-Grasmere road at NY346040 opposite a postbox in a dry-stone wall. Turn right along the road, then left at the next junction, passing a small car park before descending to the road junction at Skelwith Bridge.

5 Skelwith Bridge NY344034

The Kirkstone slate works occupy the site of a seventeenth-century corn mill. You may be able to watch craftsmen splitting the green Lakeland slate in the workshops at the back of the café.

E▶ If you don't want refreshments at the inn or the Chesters café, follow A593 (Coniston) ahead, but just before the bridge turn right between the buildings to reach a path which follows the boisterous river through roadside woods. There are viewing areas for Skelwith Force, where a fault in the greenish slate rock has formed a narrow nick down which the river plunges 16ft (5m) to a deep pool below.

The path emerges onto riverside fields. A wide path heads northwest across the fields beside the river, then by the shores of Elter Water.

6 Elter Water NY333042

Elter Water comes from the Norse 'Elptarvatn', which means 'swan's lake'. You can still see migrating whooper swans on the water. It is a shallow lake that was formed when the Great Langdale and Little Langdale glaciers, squeezed by the crags of Park Fell and Little Loughrigg, joined forces to scoop out a hollow in the softer rocks. At one time the lake would have stretched from where Elterwater village is now to Skelwith, but Great Langdale Beck and Little Langdale Beck are gradually filling it in with silt brought down from the fells. You can see their deltas to the north and south of the lake. The deltas will eventually meet, splitting the lake into two.

On Loughrigg, looking to the Langdale Pikes

▶ Beyond the lake the path turns left at the edge of woodland, then follows the river (this path sometimes becomes too wet to walk along, resulting in the use of the road back to Elterwater). On grass verges, beneath riverside sycamores, scabious, red campion and bramble grow. The track comes out on the road beside the bridge. Turn right along the road, passing through the village, then take the left fork, which leads back to the car park.

South of the main Lakes ranges, in the enclave that used to be part of Lancashire, lies the Coniston group of mountains. The most popular route here is a steep and straight climb up and down Coniston Old Man.

This is not that route. We get right in among the rock faces to ascend Dow Crag. Gentle ridgewalking leads along the tops of the eastern combes, each with its coppery-green tarn. There's a rocky crossing to Wetherlam, and a little spur called Steel Edge that might almost count as a scramble.

START/FINISH:
Coniston village (SD304975) large pay-and-display car park. At quiet times, it's possible to use the car park at the bottom of the Walna Scar Road (SD289970), taking 600ft (180m) of climb off the start of the day

DISTANCE/ASCENT:
10 miles (15.5km) / 3,900ft (1,200m)

APPROXIMATE TIME:
8½ hours

HIGHEST POINT:
Swirl How summit 2,631ft (802m)

MAP:
OS Explorer OL6;
OS Landranger 90 and 96;
Harveys Lakeland South West

REFRESHMENTS:
Coniston has three excellent pubs, as well as cafés

ADVICE:
The ascent from Goats Water onto Dow Crag is steep and difficult (and very serious under snow and ice). Stop at the tarn to eye up the line between the crags. An easier (but much less interesting) alternative is to follow the Walna Scar Road to the pass beside Brown Pike, and turn right to cross Brown Pike and follow the ridge to Dow Crag

① Coniston SD304975
'The head of the lake is an admirable junction of awful and of pleasing simplicity,' says Coleridge.

A▶ From the centre of Coniston, a small lane just left of Church Beck's bridge climbs past the Sun Inn, and past the old railway station. It then becomes very steep and narrow; there is a footpath on the left, on the far bank of a stream. After the upper car park the Walna Scar Road continues as a rough track.

② Walna Scar Road SD287970
The Walna Scar is an important route towards Ravenglass, used by Romans, pedlars, pack ponies carrying copper ore, and, unfortunately, also four-wheel drive vehicles of the present day.

B▶ Half a mile (800m) past the car park, the track passes to the right of Boo Tarn, which no longer collects water.

③ Boo Tarn SD283967
Boo Tarn is claimed as the smallest tarn in Lakeland, though to my eye Foxes Tarn on Scafell is much less large. Boo Tarn illustrates how a patch of water will gradually fill with stream silt and its own mud until it is shallow enough for rushes – after which the rushes will gather what loose dust and soil may be blowing around, then rot and die on the bottom. This process can be so rapid that tarns shown on recently published maps often turn out to not be there any more. This can be confusing if you take a bearing on one in the mist.

▶ The track crosses a stone bridge ahead, but before reaching this, turn aside at a cairn that marks steps up onto a wide, initially steep and grassy path. This heads up beside some small waterfalls to reach the foot of Goat's Water. Here stop to work out the line of the route through the crags opposite.

④ Goat's Water Foot SD266975 and Dow Crag Buttresses

Dow rhymes with 'Go' (and not with 'How'). The main buttresses are named left to right A to D, with E and F being broad and broken. Early climbing in Lakeland, based on the idea of taking an arguably rational route to some summit, followed the obvious lines of weakness: the gullies. Gullies don't make great rock climbs. They are in origin fault lines where two rock masses have moved past each other, so their rocks tend to be crushed and shattered, with shaky handholds and scree. They are damp, and slimy.

On the ridge of Dow Crag (the mountain), looking over the edge of Dow Crag (the crag). This exciting moment isn't actually a necessary part of the ridge path

Around the beginning of the last century climbers started to realise that the buttresses between the gullies were not only much nicer than the gullies, but also much easier. Each of the four buttresses has a route straight up the front on clean rock, not too steep, with good holds and splendid situations – and all at the milder grades of Difficult and Very Difficult.

On the scree below C Buttress is a group of large rocks, among which is the cave traditionally used by rock climbers for sitting in and wondering if it's worth waiting for the rain to stop. Our route will turn sharply left at this cave to the stretcher box at the bottom of B Buttress, then pass the foot of A Buttress and slant up left in an open gully behind

On the ridge of Swirl How above Levers Hawse, with Coniston Old Man and Dow Crag behind

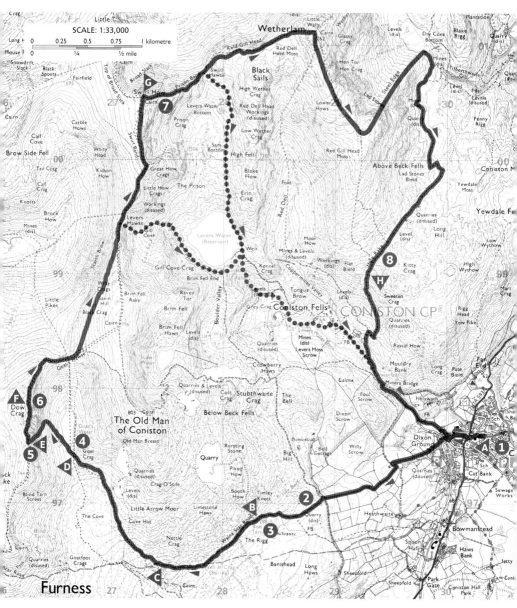

a rocky spur. The layout of the crag will be less obvious from directly underneath.

D Cross the outflow of Goat's Water on large boulders. The rough Dow Crag rocks (volcanic tuffs) are comfortable to hop over even when a brisk northerly is lifting spray from the tarn

Goat's Water and Dow Crag on a winter's afternoon

and giving the hopper a good soaking. A small path slants up to the cave, then back left to the stretcher box. Continue along the base of the crags, below the foot of Great Gully.

5 Foot of Great Gully SD263976

Starting at the bottom of the gully and going up to the right of it is an ascending shelf, not too steep and well-supplied with handholds. This is Giant's Crawl (Difficult), which for many people is their very first rock climb. It doesn't look too hard from here – and it isn't.

The shifting stones and frost-shattered ridges above are singularly inhospitable sites, unsuited to any kind of life other than humans of the hill walking sort. Combine this with subzero temperatures, long periods of lying snow, and rain that arrives too much at a time and then drains away among the boulders, and it's a wonder that any growing thing survives.

But as soon as the scree stabilises there will be the greyish matting of woolly hair moss. Where any small pockets of soil are trapped we find parsley fern, its lively green fronds frothing out from between the grey stones. The central fronds of each plant have a different leaf-form; these are the fertile fronds, and if you turn one over you'll see the spores on the underside. Most ferns have separate fertile and infertile fronds, though this doesn't apply to the commonest of them all, the bracken.

In the shelter of the gully above, where underground seepage brings minerals to the surface, alpine flowers grow: saxifrages, succulent stonecrops and rose-root, alpine lady's mantle and the familiar garden plant of the cities, London pride.

E▶ With Great Gully rising on the right, the open gully of our route now ascends ahead, with steep rock on its right and a spur of rock and grass on its left. The floor of the gully is loose stones, but a few metres up on the right are small paths, with rock handholds if needed. Our way passes the foot of Easy Gully, but continues in the (much easier) open gully ahead. Near the top our gully steepens, and small paths lead out onto the spur on the left. This is followed without difficulty to its top. Dow Crag's summit is 440yds (400m) away on the right.

⑥ Dow Crag Summit SD263977
Along the ridge there are near-vertical views down Easy Gully and Great Gully; the summit itself is even better. Stepping between the jumble of rocks that is the summit, you will suddenly see Goat's Water directly below.

F▶ The north ridge of Dow drops to Goat's Hawse. The path out of the saddle ascends steeply at first, and then a small path contours out to the left to reach Levers Hawse without further uphill. (The steep path down right, east, is an escape route back to Coniston via Levers Water.) A wide gravelly path leads northwards to Swirl How.

⑦ Swirl How NY273005
While Lakeland ridge-views are always very good, the one from the Swirl How ridge is even better than that. Behind are the Old Man and Dow, their dark shapes silhouetted against

Wetherlam (left) and Swirl How, seen from Loughrigg Fell

Morecambe Bay. The jagged cone of Harter Fell is on the left, with the sea in that direction as well. The Scafells lie ahead, while on the right are steep drops to Low Water and Levers Water, with the lakes of Coniston and Windermere lying as silver stripes across the lowlands.

G From Swirl How a fairly steep ridge called Prison Band, with rocks but a clear path between them, leads down eastwards to the pass of Swirl Hawse.

At Swirl Hawse, those who wish to shorten the walk can take a path down right, to Levers Water. From the dam, a path then goes down to left of the stream, but as the ground begins to get steeper the path crosses the stream and goes down on its right, to reach Coppermines youth hostel.

Otherwise, take the path ahead out of Swirl Hawse. After its first climb, this wanders to the left, to bypass Black Sails by crossing the top of the steep slope running down into the Greenburn valley. The path returns to the crest to reach the cairn on Wetherlam.

Descending into the Coppermines valley at the end of the walk, with Coniston Water ahead

No path descends the south ridge of Wetherlam. It gradually bends from south to southeast, and after ⅔ mile (1km) flattens briefly, with a tiny tarn (NY293003). From the tarn head northeast, to find the top of a steep and rocky spur. This is Steel Edge. Its rocks are easy-angled, and there is a small path.

The spur descends into the valley of the Crook Beck. There are paths on either side of the beck, as its valley ascends gently southwards.

8 Hole Rake NY294992
There are old mine entrances, ferny and damp, alongside the path as it approaches this little pass. Here you are suddenly confronted with the Coppermines valley: ravaged by glaciers, then ravaged again by the mines of man. And the ravagement goes on, as permission has been granted for further quarrying above the youth hostel.

H A green path zigzags down to the valley floor, where a track leads downvalley. It's best to cross Miners' Bridge, and take the older track on the right bank of Church Beck. This passes down through woods above the river, before arriving conveniently in Coniston right beside the picnic tables of the Sun Inn.

Wallowbarrow Gorge

The Duddon River wanders through oak woods before plunging into a spectacular gorge. Such places are particularly appreciated by small children, who like nothing better than the temptation to fall into the river. If they should fail to fall off the first stepping stones, this walk has another set of stepping stones later on. However, care should be taken when the river is in spate.

1 Dunnerdale SD235983

Dunnerdale is one of the least known, least walked-in valleys of Lakeland. Duddon is awkward to get to from the M6. It has hills – but they aren't very large, and they aren't in Wainwright. Its rocks are sprinkled like dragon's teeth over the entire terrain rather than raised in crag and gully. The actual valley of the Duddon, where this walk takes place, is as green and lovely as anywhere in the Lakes.

A Opposite the small car park area, a bridleway sign points downhill through bracken – it carries a warning about the stepping stones. The Fickle Steps are not stepping stones but stepping boulders and the wire hawser to hang on to is not as much help as you might suppose.

B From Fickle Steps a bridleway path signed 'Grassguards' heads straight up between the tree trunks, with Grassguards

Pink porphyry in the woods above Fickle Steps

Grassguards Gill: the second waterfall

Gill on its left. There are small outcrops in the wood (one of which is a striking pink colour), and at one point the path is carved from rock, but it is mostly on leaf mould. After a gate, the wood changes to a spruce plantation and the path is muddy for a short distance before it meets a forest road.

Turn left along the road to where it fords Grassguards Beck. There is a footbridge 22yds (20m) upstream. Continue upstream to a gate marked 'Permissive Path', to pass above Grassguards Farm and rejoin the track beyond it.

2 Grassguards SD223981

The Sawrey family, who farmed Grassguards 50 years ago, had several strapping sons; consequently the stone walls hereabouts are particularly impressive and well-built, up to 8ft (2.5m) high. At one point a wall-end broadens into a stone platform 5ft wide and 4ft high (1.5m x 1.2m) – a 'consumption dyke', built to use up stones. This indicates the back-breaking labour that went into clearing these fields.

C▷ The stony track drops a little, then rises across the slope, with views to Dow Crag and the Walna Scar road. After ²/₃ mile (1km), a house called Low Stonythwaite lies just ahead. It is built of a striking orange stone. 110yds (100m) before the house, the bridleway arrow points left, indicating a branch path.

11yds (10m) after the junction, a small path on the left leads up to the summit of Wallowbarrow Crag. A short diversion to this little-visited summit is well worthwhile, provided you don't mind the ascent of rough rocks and even rougher grass and heather. The view is straight down onto the duck pond of High Wallowbarrow farm, then on along green Dunnerdale to the sea.

Wallowbarrow Crag

Return to the main path, which zigzags downhill through a wood of oak and hazel. Above on the left are the rock climbers on Low Crag. A stream crosses the path, then runs down through the woods on the left over mossy rocks. The path leaves the wood at a gate 110yds (100m) above High Wallowbarrow farm.

3 Pink Porphyry SD221964
Back near Fickle Steps, the lowest of the Grassguards Gill waterfalls tumbled over rock that wasn't the normal Borrowdale grey but a striking reddish-orange. This stone was seen again in the walls of Stonythwaite, and in the rocks of the descending path. In this gateway, you can stand with your two feet in two different geological eras. If facing downhill, your left foot is in the Ordovician era and your right foot is about fifty million years later.

There are three ways that such a rock junction can form. The younger rock could have been squeezed in molten form as an intrusion; in this case we should see some effects of heat ('contact metamorphism') on the older rock. The two rocks could have been brought together by later earth movements; we would expect fault-line shattering along the join. Or the younger rock could have been laid as a sediment over the eroded surface of the older; in this case the younger rock would show bedding planes.

None of these signs appears here! In fact, the pink porphyry was a molten intrusion, but the dyke is a narrow one that cooled quickly, so that no chemical cooking took place in the grey lava alongside. Its rapid cooling is also shown by

High Wallowbarrow and
Dunnerdale, from
Wallowbarrow Crag

its fine-grained texture. Slow-cooled rocks, such as granite, have a coarse, crystalline structure.

D The path runs below rose bushes to High Wallowbarrow farm, which has traditional livestock: stocky Herdwick sheep, black Galloway beef cattle adapted to rough hill grazings, and a Jersey house cow. A sign 'Footpath, Seathwaite' points to the left, through the farmyard to an old green path heading east. This enters the Wallowbarrow woods through a gate. 11yds (10m) into the wood, a small path forks right, and leads to a set of fine rectangular stepping stones over the River Duddon. (The high-arched bridge, used on the return journey, is 110yds (100m) upstream.)

Once across the stepping stones, turn downstream on a riverbank footpath that leads across a footbridge into Seathwaite. The Newfield Inn is 220yds (200m) away on the left.

Directly opposite the inn, a footpath leads between farm buildings through three field gates, then crosses a field to a sign post and a wooden footbridge over Tarn Beck. A tree-root path leads back left, into an open field.

4 Peat Meadow SD228962

With the higher ground being mostly rocky and steep, and the valley bottoms drained by monastic man, Lakeland is rather short of the damp peaty ground that is so familiar to walkers in less exciting English hills.

The typical plant life of this ground is the asphodel, whose yellow flowers stand on narrow upright stalks in July and August, and the bog myrtle, a low shrub whose aromatic oval leaves can be smelt throughout summer. Bog myrtle branches were used by country people to discourage flies. It was also, along with meadowsweet, a flavouring for ale. Those who have just paid a lunch-time visit to the Newfield Inn will agree that beer made with hops is much better.

Humans need protein for body building, and plants require nitrates. In wet ground like this, nitrates get leached away. The bog myrtle and the alder tree have evolved a symbiotic relationship with nitrogen-fixing bacteria, which live inside their roots and build nitrate out of atmospheric nitrogen. Meanwhile two other wetland flowers, the sundew and the violet-coloured butterwort, get hold of their nitrate by trapping flies and midges.

▣ The path re-enters the woods, and leads to a wonderful footbridge – a high stone arch – over the Duddon. Turn right, upstream, through the Wallowbarrow Gorge.

River Duddon

River Duddon beneath
Wallowbarrow Crag

⑤ Wallowbarrow Gorge SD225967

Here the river runs through a deep wooded ravine, with crags above, and big boulders that have fallen from those crags underfoot. You'll move slowly over the jumbled boulders, when you aren't stopped altogether enjoying the view. Heather (both bell heather and ling) and ferns grow out of the tumbled boulders, while the thin soils of the oak wood support harebell, wood sorrel and cow wheat. Peregrines nest in the crags above.

The path climbs, to look down through trees onto the river, and emerges through trees.

⑥ Pen Hill SD228971

This small rocky knoll lies between road and river. The valley road runs in a hollow that seems the natural way downvalley. It seems likely that the river originally followed the road, but the glacier of the Tarn Beck blocked it and forced it to carve this alternative route.

▶ The path drops and rejoins the river. A little wooden footbridge crosses the Grassguards Gill, and now on the right are the Fickle Steps again. For excited young people, this is positively the last chance to fall in the river before returning up the bracken path to the start of the walk.

The Dunnerdale Fells

The fells of Dunnerdale don't get much attention. The map shows that they are not high enough for peak-baggers, and they are too far off the main tourist routes to get noticed. But there's another Matterhorn among these fells. It's called Stickle Pike, and, although it may only be a little Matterhorn, it's still a good peak to scramble up, to admire the magnificent view down the Duddon Valley to the Scafells.

① Ulpha SD197936
Ulpha means 'Wolf's Hill'. The village lies by the banks of the River Duddon beneath the mixed plantations of Rainsbarrow and Birks Woods and the craggy pikes of Dunnerdale. The valley was loved by Wordsworth, who devoted many sonnets to it.

A At the pull-off 270yds (250m) south of Ulpha Bridge an eastbound track heads for the cottage of Birks, at the southern tip of Birks Wood.

② Birks Wood SD201931
By these woods you may hear blackcaps, tree creepers, nuthatches or wood warblers.

B Where the track bends left to enter the woods, leave it for a path that climbs among bracken, juniper and glacier-smoothed crag. It comes to a patch of marshy grass. The wheel tracks of bikes show the way across the marsh to a waymark at its far end.

Stickle Pike from the south

START/FINISH:
270yds (250m) south of Ulpha Bridge on the Broughton in Furness road (SD196928). Roadside pull-off, also at Ulpha Bridge (SD196930) and Church (not Sundays)

DISTANCE/ASCENT:
5 miles (8km) / 1,500ft (450m)

APPROXIMATE TIME:
3 hours

HIGHEST POINT:
Stickle Pike summit 1,230ft (375m)

MAP:
OS Explorer OL6;
OS Landranger 96;
Harveys Lakeland South West

REFRESHMENTS:
On summer weekends there is an ice-cream van by the car park. Otherwise the nearest places are pubs: the Newfield Inn, Seathwaite, or the Blacksmith's Arms, Broughton Mills

ADVICE:
While all the paths exist on the ground there are places where the walker can go astray; perhaps on a shepherd's track. In summer the bracken can get high and unruly. It rarely blocks the paths but if it's wet with dew or rainfall, then you will get wet too – so take waterproof trousers

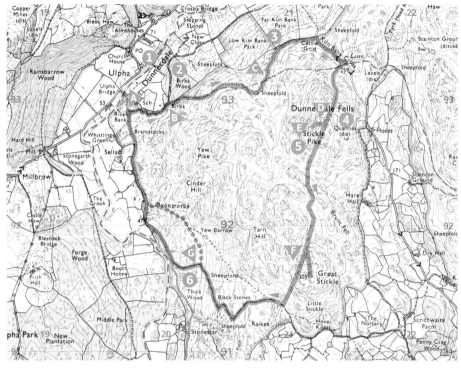

A good grass path resumes, passing through more bracken. It bears right to cross Hollow Moss Beck at a circular sheep pen and then a smaller stream. By now the craggy west sides of Stickle Pike rear up to the right.

❸ Kiln Bank SD207934

Kiln Bank's bracken-clad rocky slopes are home to the adder or viper (*Vipera berus*). Although rarely seen by most walkers, the adder is Britain's commonest reptile, with a population of about half a million. Characterised by the red eyes, the V-shaped marking at the back of the head and the dark zigzag markings from neck to tail, it rarely exceeds 2ft (60cm) in length. With heather and thick bracken for shade and rock outcrops on which to bask, the Dunnerdale Fells are an ideal habitat for this creature, as are most of the Lakeland Fells.

The adder feeds on small reptiles such as the common lizard, frogs and toads, and small mammals such as short-tailed voles. Hibernation takes place between late October and March, usually in groups and in underground dens. The males wrestle for supremacy in courtship battles during early spring.

Stickle Tarn with Stickle Pike behind

This shy snake hates being seen and will slither away when approached. Treat them with caution however. Never tantalise them or attempt to handle them. Mothers with young can be more aggressive. The adder's venom is seldom fatal; fewer than twenty cases of death have been attributed to its bites in the last one hundred years.

At SD207932 the line of the mapped bridleway becomes indistinct and the most prominent track bears left to contour north, eventually to follow a dry-stone wall that comes in from the left. This is the path marked on the OS Explorer map with black dashes. Just before reaching the tarmac lane at Kiln Bank, the track becomes choked with bracken, but a marshy pathway veers right, through bracken to reach the road. Turn right and climb along the road to the top of the pass at Kiln Bank Cross, where there are usually some parked cars.

From Kiln Bank Cross turn right on a path across grass, then take the left fork, which bends further left (south) to climb to the northern end of Stickle Tarn. The right fork is the bridleway we left at SD207932.

Stickle Tarn SD214928

This exquisite small tarn is a colourful one in summer, with the yellow of the bog asphodel and the pale pink of the bogbean contrasting with the water lilies and the greenery of rushes and reeds. It is a fascinating place where you can see dragonflies and damselflies flittering across the water and perhaps watch the ravens soaring on hillside thermals.

D Above Stickle Tarn leave the track for an eroded little path on the right. This climbs steeply to the summit of Stickle Pike.

5 Stickle Pike SD212927

Stickle Pike is not one of Lakeland's most celebrated peaks, but what it lacks in height, it makes up for in character. It has a large summit cairn, plenty of rocks to sit on, and great views down the Duddon Valley to Harter Fell, which lies ringed by the great Scafell group, Bowfell and Crinkle Crags. To the south, across more rocky bluffs, Stickle Pike's neighbour, Great Stickle, leads the eye to the sandbanks of the Duddon Estuary and the waves of Morecambe Bay.

E From Stickle Pike retrace your steps down to the track above Stickle Tarn. This grassy ribbon descends through bracken beneath Stickle Pike's scree-strewn slopes towards the conical peak of Great Stickle. The path crosses Hare Hall Beck and after a brief climb comes down to the marshy bowl at the head of Red Moss Beck. In the summer months the white tufts of cotton grass blow in the breeze. The small path runs along the slope foot, just above the right-hand edge of the marsh. Then it bends right (southeast) up a grassy hollow. At this little valley's head is a small cairn, with Great Stickle rising to the left.

F From this point you can divert up to the left to visit the trig point on Great Stickle, with a fine view southwards to the Duddon estuary. Then return, and take the continuing path, which descends quite steeply around the flank of Great Stickle, southwest.

View from Stickle Pike to the
Duddon Valley and Harter Fell

Descending into Dunnerdale from Great Stickle

In the wet hollow at the base of the hill, you meet a wide grass path running across – it's the bridleway from Broughton Mills. Turn right, and follow the green path as it wanders down roughly west. It bends gradually left, then turns back right around a small rocky knoll, descending northwest.

Stickle Pike and cotton grass

6 Stonescar Bracken SD201915

Bracken (*Pteridium aquilinum*) needs at least 8in (20cm) of soil to take hold, so you do not see it on the summits of Lakeland. On the hillsides, many of which have been covered with soils from glacial drift, it has become an invasive plant whose tall fronds smother surrounding grasses. The layers of dead fronds that are deposited means that the grasses are eradicated. The bracken spreads through a network of underground rhizomes from which new shoots sprout and unfurl in May. The replacement of cattle, who eat a certain amount of young bracken shoots and trample the rest, with sheep, who do neither, has speeded up this spread.

G On the hillside above Stonescar the path winds through bracken that gets thicker and higher with each step. Above the road there's a junction (SD203917). The bridleway path turns left, downhill, to join the road where the river is close alongside it. But outside high summer with its heavy bracken, keep ahead on a contouring path, which gradually drops to join the road 1/3 mile (600m) further north. Either way, follow the road up-valley to the start.

Ravenglass & Muncaster Fell

START:
Car park at Ravenglass (SD085965) or park in Eskdale Green and take your train ride before your walk

FINISH:
Irton Road Station (SD137999)

DISTANCE/ASCENT:
5¼ miles (8.5km) / 800ft (250m)

APPROXIMATE TIME:
3 hours

HIGHEST POINT:
Hooker Crag, Muncaster Fell 758ft (231m)

MAP:
OS Explorer OL6;
OS Landranger 96

REFRESHMENTS:
Ratty Arms, Ravenglass.
Teas at Ravenglass & Eskdale Railway Station, Ravenglass

This short linear route follows a section of the Lakeland to Lindisfarne long distance way. It starts on the seashore at Ravenglass, discovers a little-known castle, then climbs to one of Lakeland's best 'little' hills. And when the walking is done, you just hop on 'L'aal Ratty', a narrow-gauge railway with steam engines.

1 Ravenglass SD085965

The Romans came to Cumbria in the first century AD, and built a fort, Glannaventa, to the south of Ravenglass. This was one of many guarding the Cumbrian coast. The forts were an extension to those of Hadrian's Wall, which ended at Bowness-on-Solway. Ravenglass was to become the Romans' regional naval base. The Romans then built a road through the Lakeland hills linking Glannaventa with Galava (at Waterhead), passing through high Eskdale to the remote Fort of Hardknott (see Walk 10).

Ravenglass continued to flourish as a port until the Industrial Revolution. It was once infamous for its smugglers.

A Go over the main railway station's footbridge, then round behind the station of the narrow-gauge railway. It's well worth taking the time to see 'Ratty's' little steam engines.

The beach at Ravenglass

One of Ratty's little trains

The gravel path past the little station comes to a junction close to the road (SD087965). Turn right along a track with a public footpath signpost. The tarmac track runs south past a caravan site into a narrow strip of woodland. Here there's a gravel path alongside on the left. Path and track lead to the ruins of the Roman bathhouse.

❷ Walls Castle SD088959
Today all that remains of the Roman fort of Glannaventa is the bathhouse, yet this red sandstone building with 12ft- (3.5m-) walls is one of the best preserved Roman buildings in Northern England.

▶ About 110yds (100m) beyond the bathhouse, take the rougher left fork in the tracks before Walls Mansion. Leave the track before Newtown for a rougher track, signed for Muncaster on the left, which heads northeast through the decorative woodlands and rhododendron thickets of the Muncaster Castle estate – the castle itself cannot be seen from the path.

❸ Muncaster Castle SD103965
Muncaster Castle is surrounded by beautiful woods and gardens filled with colourful rhododendrons and azaleas. The pele tower dates back to the fourteenth century and stands on Roman foundations. The castle was extended throughout the following centuries; much of it, including the more modern tower, was built in the mid-nineteenth century by Anthony Salvin, an architect well known for 'modernising' castles.

The castle has been in the hands of the Pennington family since 1325. Henry VI sheltered here in 1464, following his

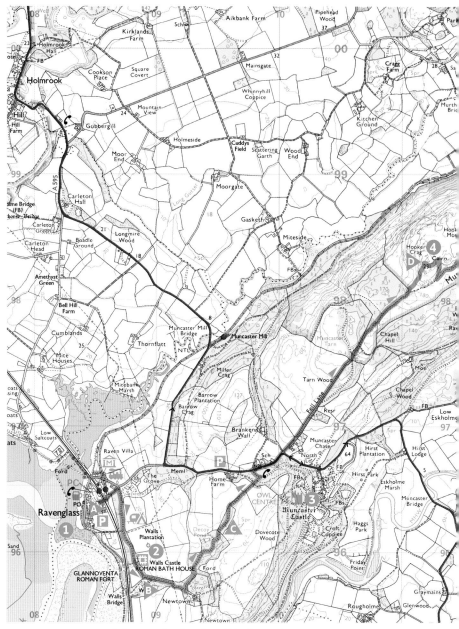

defeat at the Battle of Hexham. According to legend he was led down from Muncaster Fell by a local shepherd and rested for nine days. In gratitude he left his drinking bowl behind. This glass bowl, decorated with gold and enamel, is known as

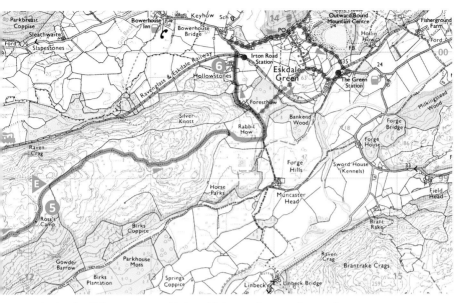

the Luck of Muncaster and it is said that as long as it remains intact the Penningtons will live and thrive in the place.

C▸ Beyond the Decoy Pond, the track continues northeast, soon between fields. Beyond a couple of gates it enters some more woods. Here the right-of-way turns left towards Home Farm, but a permissive path (Esk TR) lets you keep ahead to Muncaster Castle's entry hut. Bear left through a stone arch to the A595.

Turn right for 330yds (300m), and where the road bends to the right, continue ahead up a wide stony track, marked 'Muncaster Fell via Fell Lane'. The lane climbs northeast with woods on its right, and glimpses of Eskdale behind.

The track dips into trees. Ignore a left fork, and keep ahead to a signpost with Muncaster Tarn now visible through trees on the left. At the signpost, as the bridleway turns down to the right towards High Eskholme, keep ahead on a rougher track uphill. After a gate, it enters the world of fell and mountain, and shrinks to a path that climbs among rocky outcrops and bracken to Hooker Crag's summit trig point.

4 Muncaster Fell (Hooker Crag) SD112983
The rocky summit is crowned by a trig point. From here you can look west to the Cumbrian coastline. The chequered pattern of farm fields and copses is dissected by the estuaries

Eskdale and Harter Fell from
Muncaster Fell

and meandering courses of the Rivers Esk and Mite. In the
distance the outlines of Sellafield remind us of issues we
would rather forget. Down in Eskdale, the narrowing sliver of
green that surrounds the meandering river weaves through
the crusty crags and bluffs that rise to Harter Fell. In the
opposite direction the soaring whaleback of Illgill Head leads
the eye to Scafell and the high western peaks.

D The long ridge ahead has various paths that come and go.
The marked bridleway line is probably the best of the paths
and passes the Victorian cromlech at Ross's Camp. To find it,
carry on down Hooker Crag's summit hump northeast, but
at its base turn sharply back right, south, on a path down a
little hollow. It slants through bracken to meet the bridleway
path, where you turn sharply back left (east). In 55yds (50m),
fork left (northeast), soon passing the broken remains of a
small sandstone pillar lying in the heather.

The path follows the southern flank of the moorland ridge,
looking down on the Esk River. After about ¼ mile (400m)
it takes a sharp diversion up left to avoid some swamp.
Resuming its line along the top of the south-facing flank, the
path reaches Ross's Camp.

5 Ross's Camp SD121987
The slab of rock placed on three boulders is known as Ross's
Camp. Ross worked for the Muncaster Estate at the end of
the nineteenth century, but the origins of this construction
are a mystery. Some historians believe it was used as a
shelter for labourers working on the old road; others think it
was a picnic table for shooting parties.

▶ Now Eskdale Green is in sight, surrounded by mixed woodland and the rough crags of Fell End. The path bends left, right across the hill, running due north to get around another swamp. It meets a wider path, where you turn down right, northeast again, to a gateway at the corner of a wall.

The path runs down to right of the wall, but eases away from it to cross the col before the final hump of Silver Knott. The path, now terraced and firm, contours around the right flank of Silver Knott, and drops east to a wall with kissing gate at the hill base. A clear earth path soon leads to a crossing track. Turn left, waymarked as bridleway. After a brief descent, a footpath turns off right, and could be used to reach The Green station. Otherwise keep ahead, through a gate, to pass Forest How. The lane, now tarmac, leads down to cross the narrow gauge railway at Irton Road station. If there's time to spare you could follow the road round to the village of Eskdale Green, where there's a post office selling sandwiches, ice cream and chocolate.

⑥ The Ravenglass and Eskdale Railway SD137999
The old steam-driven railway that chugs all the way up Eskdale to Boot was constructed in 1875 as a 3ft- (1m-) gauge line to convey iron ore. It was converted in 1915 to a 15in- (38cm-) gauge. When the mine closed, Ratty was used to carry passengers and pink Eskdale granite from the quarries at Beckfoot. In 1960 there was a threat of closure. However, it was purchased by the Preservation Society, with the help of Colin Gilbert and Lord Wakefield. It has since operated as a tourist attraction, and will now carry you in style back to Ravenglass.

Descending from Muncaster Fell to Eskdale Green

Hampsfell

START/FINISH:
Grange-over-Sands railway station (SD412781). Car park at foot of Windermere Road (SD412783) and in Grange centre

DISTANCE/ASCENT:
4½ miles (7km) / 800ft (250m)

APPROXIMATE TIME:
3 hours

HIGHEST POINT:
Hampsfell summit 735ft (224m)

MAP:
OS Explorer OL7;
OS Landranger 96 or 97

REFRESHMENTS:
Grange-over-Sands

ADVICE:
The valuable Hampsfell Nature Trail booklet, published by Grange and District Natural History Society, is obtainable in Grange for about £1

Hampsfell, above Grange-over-Sands, is not a Lakeland hill. At 735ft (224m) it's not much of a hill; you can be up it in twenty minutes, even starting, as you have to, at sea level. And it's not Lakeland. In Lakeland you stand on grey scree, and look at lumpy fells and at lakes. On Hampsfell you can stand on herb rich turf or limestone pavement and have glorious panoramic views of mountains, fells and the sea or sand.

1 Grange-over-Sands SD412781

Grange actually belongs to the far south; it's a transported corner of Devon or Cornwall. Palm trees grow in its gardens, tea shops flourish right through to November, and you may well want to eat an ice cream. The difference is the sea, which, instead of Cornwall's boring blue stuff, offers miles of gleaming mud, and Lancashire on the other side.

A Turn left out of the station forecourt, and at once right on the B5271 (Windermere Road) leading out of the town. It climbs gently, to reach a footpath on the left after 330yds (300m). This is signed for Routen Well and Hamsfield. After 55yds (50m) it crosses a driveway and 220yds (200m) later, another. Opposite, one path bears left and another goes straight up, but they soon rejoin and continue uphill through Eggerslack Woods. Waymarks are now signed for Hampsfell.

Just above Eggerslack Woods, the first view to the main Lakeland Fells

Limestone pavement on Hampsfell, view to Morecambe Bay

② Eggerslack Wood SD412785

Straight away you start to see limestone pavement. Under a thin covering of leaf mould, white limestone rock has been scraped bare by glaciers. Here and there on the limestone lie boulders of a quite different, greyish rock; these are lumps of Silurian slate, carried in from the north by the glacier. Limestone soils are thin, but fertile. The wood supports many lime-loving wild flowers, particularly enjoyable in the spring. The main ground cover is dog's mercury and ramsons (wild garlic), with wood anemone, primrose, bluebell and early purple orchid.

Birds worth looking out for are sparrowhawk, tree creeper, nuthatch and hawfinch, as well as the common woodland species such as wrens, thrushes, woodpeckers and jays.

▶ After ½ mile (800m) the path reaches some water supply tanks, fenced in with railings.

③ Eggerslack Yews SD407790

Yews grow in many parts of Lakeland, but particularly appreciate limestone woods. Several fine and ancient ones grow around the water tanks. The yew is not a conifer, as it bears small red fruits. The fruit is designed to be eaten by birds, but all other parts of the tree are poisonous. Even the seed, designed to pass through the bird undamaged, is poisonous if crushed. As little as 6oz (150g) of the foliage has been enough to kill a horse, although deer can eat yew without harm.

The close-grained wood is excellent for making small turned items. The traditional English longbow was carved out along the junction of the springy sapwood and the strong, resilient heartwood.

C▶ The path steepens for a while, then emerges onto open fell at a stile. Limestone boulders on the right are a viewpoint to the Eastern Fells. The main path slants up to the left signposted 'The Hospice'; it is faint, but there are waymarks.

Pass to the left, below a low limestone cliff. As the ground steepens, pass between two sycamore trees to a wall stile. Follow the wall to the right for 55yds (50m), to a corner.

The square building at the summit of Hampsfell is now ahead, but it's worth turning half-right at the wall corner to visit an impressive area of limestone pavement.

Final approach to Hampsfell summit and the Hospice

4 Hampsfell Limestone SD400795

The glacier left a bare scraped surface, but water dissolves limestone to form the distinctive deep cracks called 'grykes'. The remaining upstanding lumps are 'clints'. The soil in the gryke bottoms is fertile, but shady, and supports various ferns such as hart's tongue and spleenwort. Flowering plants that flourish with such low light levels are woodland ones: dog's mercury, nettle, herb Robert and enchanter's nightshade. Thorn trees, with juniper and the occasional sycamore, have also established themselves here, where their young saplings are safe from the nibbling of sheep and rabbits.

▶ 220yds (200m) to the south is the Hospice, which marks the summit of Hampsfell.

5 Hampsfell Summit SD399794

The Hospice was built, two hundred years ago, as a shelter for travellers. From here, far across the mud of Morecambe Bay, the flat top of Ingleborough can sometimes be seen in the southwest. But the finest views from this side are northward, past the limestone scars of Whitbarrow, to the Lakeland fells. Quite likely the Lakeland fells are in cloud, making you glad you fled to the sunny South for the day. If they are in sight, it'll be hard to work out which is which; this is not where you normally see them from. For that particular problem, help is at hand.

On the roof of the Hospice is a useful apparatus, a circular viewfinder identifying all the salient features. These include the Pennines, the Howgills, the Lakeland mountains and, occasionally, the Welsh Mountains. For testing your skill with the compass, take the bearing of a distant fell. 'Magnetic to

Looking across the Kent Estuary from Hampsfell, showing Arnside and Arnside Knott

grid subtract' so subtract 5 degrees, and swing the wooden arm of the apparatus to the number indicated. If you got the bearing right, the pointer will now be pointing at your chosen fell, and the notice board will tell you the name of it. And if you got it wrong, you should be doubly relieved that you aren't wandering about on those distant misted mountains.

E ▶ The south west route down Hampsfell is along a limestone ridge covered in short turf and offers the mildest of walking. Bear south on the public footpath from the Hospice and pass a sprawling cairn before climbing over a stile in a wall. Follow the path until it passes through a broken wall. In 275yds (250m) the path divides. Take the right hand fork and at a thorn tree and waymark continue uphill. After about ¼ mile (400m) there is a gateway and adjacent stile. At this point the public footpath turns left, but to enjoy views over the Furness Fells and Cartmel continue ahead up the gradual climb to the cairn at Fell End, with extensive views to the west.

Keep ahead past the cairn, then bear gradually left between gorse bushes towards houses below. At the corner of a golf course just before the houses, turn right down a farm lane to the road below. Turn right along the fairly busy road for 65yds (60m), to find a hidden ladder stile in the hedge on the left. A path runs down the field below and through a wood to turn down a quieter road into Grange.

After ½ mile (800m) go straight across the B5277 Allithwaite Road, and down Cart Lane opposite, to reach the railway. A path signed 'Promenade' runs to the left and then under the railway line.

⑥ Morecambe Bay SD408773

Alongside the promenade, at least when the tide is out, are the wide mud flats of Morecambe Bay, partly covered in spartina grass. For Wordsworth this was the best way into the Lakes from Lancashire, with the Coniston Fells rising surprisingly out of the mud. The dangers of the shifting channels and quicksand, which claimed many lives and sometimes whole stagecoaches, were preferable to the long and stony roads via Kendal.

Walkers today are led across by the Queen's Guide, Cedric Robinson of Grange. Some years ago he escorted the Duke of Edinburgh and several horse-drawn carriages.

A black block on the distant shoreline is the nuclear power station at Heysham: It is only 12 miles (19km) away, but looks appropriately huge, distant and sinister, particularly with a wide mud foreground. Blackpool Tower, 40 miles (64km) away, can also be seen.

▶ After about ½ mile (800m) cross the railway by a level crossing, and head up a steep lane. At the top, turn right (signed Kendal) down the Main Street to reach the cafés of Grange. If time is short, simply continue along the seafront and return to the station through the underpass.

The Coniston Fells from Hampsfell

START/FINISH:
Roadside pulloff at NY210011; parking place at NY213011

DISTANCE/ASCENT:
8½ miles (13.5km) / 3,000ft (900m)

APPROXIMATE TIME:
7 hours

HIGHEST POINT:
Scafell summit 3,163ft (964m)

MAP:
OS Explorer OL6;
OS Landranger 89 or 90;
Harveys Lakeland West

TRANSPORT:
Lakeside and Haverthwaite Railway; Steamer: Coniston Launch, National Trust Gondola; Windermere Lake Cruises

REFRESHMENTS:
Woolpack Inn 1½ miles (2.25km) west, and further down Eskdale at Boot and Eskdale Green

ADVICE:
The path up Scafell is easily lost, with crags alongside, and the descent route is between crags. The only escape routes are highly inconvenient ones to Wasdale. A serious route, even in summer, to be undertaken only by those with hill experience and skills. After heavy rain the Esk River may be impossible to ford: don't attempt to pass below Green Crag, but use a path running south from the first big bend of the river (NY221046)

Scafell is the National Park's wildest mountain, and Upper Eskdale its wildest valley. This is a walk among crags through fairly remote country.

❶ Eskdale NY213014
No valley changes its character so radically as Eskdale does at Brotherilkeld. Lower Eskdale has oak woods, a golden river and a charming little railway. But at the foot of the Hardknott Pass the river turns north, and becomes a gorge; at the head of the gorge is a broad boggy place surrounded by crags and high mountains.

There are many Esk rivers, others being in the North York Moors, Dumfriesshire and the Eastern Grampians. The British 'uisce' simply means 'water'.

Ⓐ▶ At the phone box (NY212012) follow the entrance track of Brotherilkeld Farm, forking left just before the buildings to a footbridge with a sign 'Scafell'. A path leads to a kissing gate at Taw House farm. Now a track leads to the right for ½ mile (800m) to a ladder stile and gate onto the open hill.

Straight away a small path ascends in sweeping zigzags through the bracken. Before the slope eases and the bracken becomes less troublesome, the path splits and fades into the

Brotherilkeld Farm at the entrance to Upper Eskdale is the walk's start

bog. Just keep uphill, parallel with Catcove Beck, to join a clear path with cairns. This is followed to the right, passing just above the very top of Catcove Beck's gorge.

B Above the gorge, Catcove Beck forms a wide bog, and the path keeps to firm ground to the left of this. Then it rises gradually northwards onto the southern spur of Scafell. A boulder beside the path has a low overhang which shows red stains of the 'smit' used to mark sheep: it rubs off the sheep onto the rock when they shelter here.

The path swings to the left to avoid the outcrops of Horn Crag. However, scrambling straight up the clean, easy rocks is an enjoyable way to gain the little rocky summit of Slight Side.

② Slight Side NY210050

Out to the west, the strange shapes of Sellafield nuclear power station will soon stand out against the Irish Sea. Few in West Cumbria are anti-nuclear; Sellafield and its accompanying research laboratories are the principal employers in an area devastated by the closing of coal mines. Even Joss Naylor, Wasdale shepherd and famous fell-runner, worked at Sellafield for several years.

The ridge of Scafell: looking down from Long Green to Burnmoor Tarn and the sea

These stony wastes above the 2,500ft (750m) contour support little wildlife. The bird of the mountains, the raven, flies the updraughts alongside the ridges, and nests in the high crags. It may often be seen riding the wind through the narrow gap of Mickledore. Any crow-like bird flying confidently this high will be a raven; the identification can be confirmed by its deep, croaking call, and by the tail, which comes to a blunt point where the crow's tail is fanned.

C The ridge narrows, rises to the top called Long Green, and becomes stony with occasional rock outcrops, before reaching Scafell's summit cairn.

Do not attempt to descend directly to Foxes Tarn from the summit. Follow a cairned path northeast for 160yds (150m) into a shallow col, where a cross of stones lies on the ground. Now note the cairned path descending sharply on the right: this will be the descent route. However, first go forward another 55yds (50m) to the brink of Scafell Crag. To the right of the rock knoll of Symonds Knott, you peer across at the out-jutting Scafell Pinnacle. Continue up a slight rise, to gaze across to Scafell Pike.

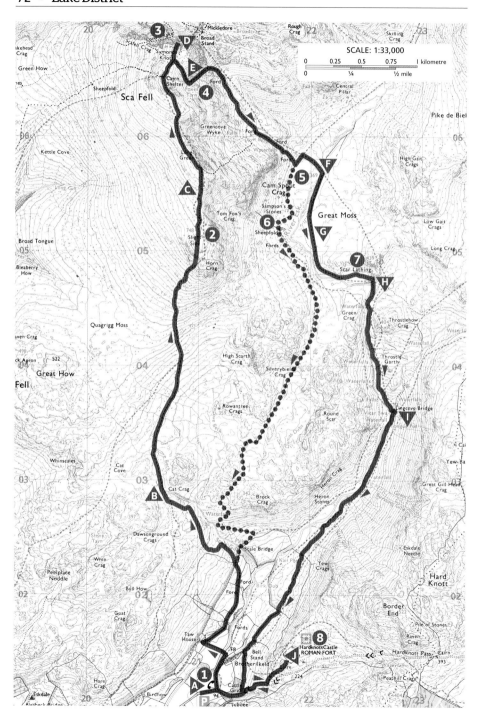

Scafell summit cairn

3 Scafell Crag NY208067

You can appreciate the difficulties of any direct descent from here to Mickledore, the narrow col leading to Scafell Pike. Here on 5 August 1802, the poet Coleridge sat on a convenient stone writing about his surroundings to his beloved Sara Hutchinson (whose sister later married Wordsworth). He tucked the letter in his pocket half-finished, and set about finding a way down to Mickledore.

'When I find it convenient to descend from a mountain, I am too confident and too indolent to look round about and wind about till I find a track. The first place I came to, that was not direct rock, I slipped down, and went on for a while with tolerable ease – but now I came (it was midway down) to a smooth perpendicular rock about 7ft high – this was nothing. I put my hands on the ledge, and dropped down.' After several such drops, he realised that he ought to turn back, but that the cliffs he had dropped over were impossible to climb. At last he found himself on the sloping shelf half way down the rock climb now called Broad Stand, 100ft (30m) above the screes of Mickledore. 'My limbs were all in a tremble – I was beginning according to my custom to laugh at myself for a madman, when the sight of the crags above me, and the impetuous clouds just over them, posting so rapidly and impetuously northwards, overawed me. I lay in a state of almost prophetic trance and delight.'

Looking round the corner to the left, he discovered the fissure (Fat Man's Agony) that leads safely down to Mickledore. His descent is the earliest rock climb recorded in the Fell & Rock Club guidebooks.

Waterfalls of the Esk River

D Don't descend from here, but return to the col with the cross of stones. Take the steeply descending path on the left (southeast) already noted. If the path is in a state of disrepair take care on the descent as there may be unstable scree underfoot. It leads to Foxes Tarn.

④ Foxes Tarn NY209064
We think of mountain landscapes as immutable, but all the boulder field beyond the tarn formed during a single cloudburst in September 1958, and the same storm was responsible for the present small size of the tarn itself. With its tiny patch of lawn, almost encircled by great crags and screes, it is considered the smallest tarn in England and also the second highest (after Broadcrag Tarn on Scafell Pike).

E A small path follows the outflow from the tarn. After 3 minutes of descent, cairns lead left, away from the stream, to the top of a boulder gully. The boulders are well-jammed, and the clamber down the gully is not difficult, although perhaps a little tricky in the wet.

The gully leads into a little descending valley under Scafell Pike. A path goes down beside the right-hand of two streams in the valley. The stream drops over the Cam Spout waterfalls. The path scrambles down bare, slippery rock to left of the stream to reach the floor of Eskdale.

⑤ Upper Eskdale NY219058
In 1936 the Forestry Commission proposed to extend its plantations from Ennerdale into this upper valley. They argued that it was not really Lakeland as it has no lake. Opponents of the scheme successfully pointed out that Great Langdale does not have a lake either – though any visitor to this crag-circled hollow will be able to think of even better reasons not to turn it over to the production of wood pulp.

News of another scheme for a full-blown ski resort with chairlifts and cafés and an access road caused some alarm a few years ago. The date this proposal was published happened to be 1 April.

F Cross the flat valley floor, and the River Esk, to a path on its left bank, and turn downstream. After very heavy rain the Esk River may be impossible to ford: don't attempt to pass below Green Crag, but use a path running south from the first big bend of the river (it starts at a sheepfold NY221050 and heads south).

6 Sampson Stones NY218054

These stones were not brought by any Biblical strongman, but gradually broke off the face of Cam Spout Crag as a result of water getting into cracks behind and then freezing. The same frost action causes the shattered stones of the high summits. Caught in a storm, after his descent of Broad Stand, Coleridge took these large boulders to be peat-hovels. However, they weren't, so he found shelter in a sheepfold and eventually escaped from the storm at Taw House, near the start of our walk. His walk, over ten days, had brought him from Keswick by Buttermere and Ennerdale Water to St Bees and then back to Wastdale. After spending a day with John Towers, the farmer of Taw House, he continued by Devoke Water to Broughton Mills and Coniston, returning home by Grasmere.

G The path stays on the left-hand side of the River Esk throughout.

7 Scar Lathing NY225047

Here the river turns sharply right and drops into its gorge. On the upper pastures, sheep suppress almost everything except grass and bracken. Down in the gorge, though, you will find birch, alder, rowan and willow, and many wild flowers such as golden rod, harebell, scabious and saxifrage.

H The path runs down alongside the gorge – there is also a path on the west (right-hand) side of the river, but that one is narrow, exposed and loose.

I The path crosses the Lingcove Beck on an old packhorse bridge. At the first field wall, marking the boundary of National Trust land, is a ladder stile. Here keep ahead slightly uphill to a gate and ladder stile (while the main path turns down slightly right to rejoin the stream). A track leads towards Brotherilkeld, but just before the farm bear up left, above a wood, to a ladder stile onto the Hardknott road.

To reach the Roman fort, turn left up the road for ¼ mile (400m) as it starts to climb the Hardknott Pass. A signed footpath branches off left up a grassy spur.

8 Mediobogdum (Hardknott Castle) NY218014

The Roman fort of Mediobogdum is well worth visiting, especially in the evening when long shadows lie across the civilising signs of centuries more recent than the second century AD.

Hardknott Fort, looking through the North Gate to Scafell

Military cutbacks meant a retreat from southern Scotland and a shift from aggressive mobile forces to a more defensive strategy. Under the emperor Hadrian the famous Wall was built, and behind it forts were hardened up, with stonework replacing wood. Mediobogdum guarded the Hardknott Pass and provided a safe overnight stop on the strategic road from the port of Ravenglass to Penrith and the Roman main road along the line of the present-day M6. It was manned by auxiliaries of the fourth cohort from Dalmatia, in the Balkans. The impressive stone walls, about 16½ft (5m) high, had fallen almost to ground level but have now been partly rebuilt. They enclose about 12 acres (5 hectares), enough to house 1,000 men. Permanent stone buildings inside the walls were the granary, commandant's house and administrative block. The foundations of these survive and are marked with signs. Wooden buildings, now lost, will have included barrack blocks, with guard houses at the four gateways, and latrines and stables against the wall.

▶ Return down the steep path to the road and car park.

Scafell Pike

The climb from Wasdale to Scafell Pike via Mickledore is a hard and steep one, but it rewards you with awe-inspiring views of Scafell Crag. It is combined with a descent via Esk Hause and Sty Head for a very satisfying day on England's highest mountain.

1 Wastwater NY178071
Wastwater is different to the other lakes of Lakeland. It's deeper, colder and purer, but is also more sterile. There is little that can eke out a living in its waters except the arctic char. The char has been here since the Ice Age, and spawns in the bitterly cold waters between November and March.

Lingmell Beck, which brings down the rains and snows from the high peaks, brings down their boulders too. The wide boulder beds are scattered with yellow-flowered gorse, quite a spectacle on stormy days when the cliffs of the Scafells glower down, black and threatening.

A▶ Cross the concrete bridge over Lingmell Gill. On the opposite side a signpost points out the concessionary path along the right-hand bank of the gill. This path meets the right of way from Wastwater Screes just before Brackenclose, a Fell and Rock Climbing Club hut. The surrounding lower slopes are scattered with broad-leafed trees and bracken, but above them the route can be seen entering a shady hollow, the world of rock and the Scafells.

START/FINISH:
Car park at the camp site near Brackenclose, Wasdale Head (NY182075)

DISTANCE/ASCENT:
8 miles (13km) / 3,300ft (1,000m)

APPROXIMATE TIME:
7 hours

HIGHEST POINT:
Scafell Pike 3,209ft (978m)

MAP:
OS Explorer OL6;
OS Landranger 89 or 90
Harveys Lakeland West

REFRESHMENTS:
Wasdale Head Inn

ADVICE:
This is dangerous country when bad or unsettled weather prevails. In several places, especially around Esk Hause and Sty Head, the inexperienced or ill-equipped walker could become hopelessly lost. It is essential to carry a map and compass and to know how to use them

Mickledore and Scafell Crag

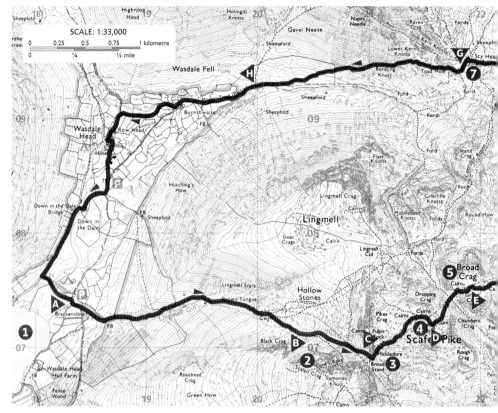

The path recrosses the stream on a wooden footbridge and continues on a steady climb along the northern banks.

The stream is crossed once more and a bold, engineered path of pitched boulders (slippery in wet weather) continues over Brown Tongue, penetrating ever deeper into the shady confines of Hollow Stones. Here among the rocks and grass are carpets of bilberries.

As you gain height, the vertical cliffs of Scafell's northern face become more and more imposing and you can look up the narrow cleft of Lord's Rake, a popular and exciting route to this summit.

❷ Scafell Crag NY205068
While Scafell Pike's Pulpit Rock is sunlit and friendly, with easy rock climbs, the brooding cliffs of Scafell Crag are at most times of the day sunless. On this black cliff are some of Lakeland's most challenging climbing routes.

B▶ Our route, however, continues through Hollow Stones towards Mickledore, the col between Scafell and the Pike. The way is now steeper, and the terrain consists of loose red screes, then a little gully. The difficulties are shortlived, however, and you are soon at Mickledore, one of the great Lakeland passes.

❸ Mickledore NY210069

In his classic guide of 1902, *The Lake Counties*, W.G. Collingwood described Mickledore thus: 'The two separate mountains of Scafell and the Scafell Pikes are like two castle towers, between which would be a clear course but for a little gatehouse filling the gap. The gatehouse has a ridged roof, one end of which rests against the side of each tower. The northern tower, Scafell Pikes, has been so battered at the top that you can clamber down its ruined upper storey and get upon the ridge of the gatehouse roof. Then you are in Mickledore, the great gap: but when you have ridden the rough roof beam like an Icelandic ghost, and reach the other side, thinking to climb the southern tower, Scafell, you find that it is not nearly so ruined.'

Indeed it isn't. You have seen the main crag on the way up. Now there is East Buttress, with its fine climbs on the Overhanging Wall, Mickledore Chimney and Broad Stand. Collingwood's 'rough roof beam' leads to the slabs of Broad Stand, the scene of Samuel Taylor Coleridge's 'first rock climb' (see Walk 10).

C▶ From Mickledore turn left to climb on a cairned path over boulder-strewn slopes to the summit of Scafell Pike.

❹ Scafell Pike NY215073

A gigantic circular cairn, now crumbling, and a stone-built trig point top a boulder-ridden summit with little life on it except for lichens and ravens, and of course people – the top of England is always a favourite with people.

As would be expected from the highest place in England the views are magnificent, especially from the edges. Possibly the finest is that to the north and west, where the domed massif of Great Gable gets its elbows in front of Pillar and Kirkfell.

On Broad Crag, with Scafell Pike behind

Descend east from Scafell Pike's summit. After precisely 55yds (50m) – no further or you reach the edge of the cliff – you will come to a cairned path that heads northeast across bouldery terrain. The path drops more steeply into Broad Crag Col, a narrow gap separating Piers Gill (left) and Little Narrowcove (right). Now the stony path clambers up again onto the east shoulder of Broad Crag, missing the summit cairn by a mere 110yds (100m).

⑤ Broad Crag NY218076
Though a three-thousand footer (814m), Broad Crag does not have enough descent on all sides to merit being classed as a separate peak. Wainwright was most unkind in his assessment: 'arid – an outcast, unloved, except by foxes.'

Descend to another narrow saddle of land, then climb onto the shoulder of Ill Crag. The path sticks to the Wasdale side of the fell and gives striking views over the edge and across Great End's crags to Sty Head Tarn and Great Gable.

On the approach to Great End, the path veers right (east) and descends beneath its eastern scree slopes towards Esk Hause, a confusing meeting point for routes from Langdale, Wasdale, Eskdale and Borrowdale.

Just before the hause, watch out for a path on the left (NY232081), which descends north to the big wide path between Angle Tarn and Sprinkling Tarn. It's marked by faint black slashes on the OS Explorer map and black dashes on the Harveys maps.

Near a cross-shaped stone shelter turn left along this path, descending beneath the dark cliffs of Great End and by the shaly ravine of Ruddy Gill. Ruddy Gill turns right on its way to Borrowdale, but here fork left on a path that continues northwest, soon to skirt the southern shores of Sprinkling Tarn.

6 Sprinkling Tarn NY228092

Sprinkling Tarn is the dramatic setting for a fight to the death in Hugh Walpole's *Rogue Herries*. David Herries and his sweetheart Sarah were fleeing Wasdale and the attentions of her evil uncle, Denburn, and her fiancé, Captain Bann. The two villains caught up with them near Sty Head Tarn, on a night when the moon dodged in and out of a swirling mist.

After a frenzied sword fight, David injured the Captain's arm. But Denburn joined the fray, climbing into the night for a more advantageous position by Sprinkling Tarn. David parted Denburn from his sword, but soon Denburn had him in a murderous stranglehold and the life appeared to be draining from David's limbs. He reeled, and the grip was broken. David tossed his assailant into the tarn, where he drowned.

▶ Soon after leaving Sprinkling Tarn behind, Sty Head Tarn comes into view, cowering in a grassy hollow beneath Great

Bowfell seen from
Scafell Pike's summit

Kirk Fell and Great Gable from Esk Hause

Gable. The path does not aim for this but veers west for the pass above and to the left of it. Here it meets the wide Wasdale-Borrowdale path that straddles the pass at the foot of Gable.

⑦ Sty Head NY219095

In past centuries trains of Galloway ponies loaded with graphite from Borrowdale and slate from Honister were led over Sty Head, bound for Wasdale, Langdale or the port at Ravenglass. The returning traders may have brought luxury items such as tobacco or brandy: some legal, some smuggled.

G▶ Near a box containing a rescue stretcher turn left to descend the middle slopes of Great Gable into Wasdale. The path passes through spectacular scenery, with the crags of Lingmell and the rocky gash of Piers Gill prominent on the left.

H▶ Eventually the route descends to the northern banks of Lingmell Beck, which it traces to the rough pastures of upper Wasdale. After keeping Burnthwaite Farm to the left the path traces Fog Mire Beck, crossing it and recrossing it several times using little log bridges. Beneath the bracken slopes at the foot of Kirk Fell, the path meets Mosedale Beck and follows it past the little packhorse bridge into the village of Wasdale Head. Turn left by the Wasdale Head Inn then right along the tarmac lane, back to the car park.

Mosedale Horseshoe

The Mosedale Horseshoe is one of the Lakeland classics – a high-level route taking in several fine summits, including Pillar, Steeple and Yewbarrow. The excitement can be heightened by taking the Pillar High-level path to visit Pillar Rock.

1 Wasdale Head NY187087

Wasdale is a small farming community that has gradually turned its hand to catering for walkers and climbers, and is centred on the large inn that was run during the nineteenth century by Will Ritson. Auld Will was a larger-than-life character who boasted of his exploits on the hills and told tall stories about crossing foxes with eagles and producing flying foxes. A 'biggest-liar' competition is still run at the Bridge Inn in nearby Santon Bridge.

The tiny St Olaf's Church, surrounded by yews, has huge roof slates supported by beams said to have been salvaged from the wreckage of a Viking ship. One of the windows has an etching of Napes Needle and the words 'I will lift up mine eyes unto the hills from whence cometh my strength'. In the churchyard are memorials to Himalayan climbers and the graves of many who lost their lives on the local fells.

A From the car park, walk up the road to the village, then turn left past the Wasdale Head Inn. Beyond the hotel, turn right alongside Mosedale Beck passing, but not crossing the

START/FINISH:
Car park at Wasdale Head
NY187084

DISTANCE/ASCENT:
10 miles (16km) / 3,900ft
(1,200m)

APPROXIMATE TIME:
6-7 hours

HIGHEST POINT:
Pillar 2,927ft (892m)

MAP:
OS Explorer OL4 and OL6;
OS Landranger 89
Harveys Lakeland West

REFRESHMENTS:
Wasdale Head Inn

ADVICE:
A serious walk with a couple of short exposed sections. Only experienced walkers should attempt this in wintry conditions, and then only when equipped with ice axes and crampons

Walking up Mosedale with Pillar in the background

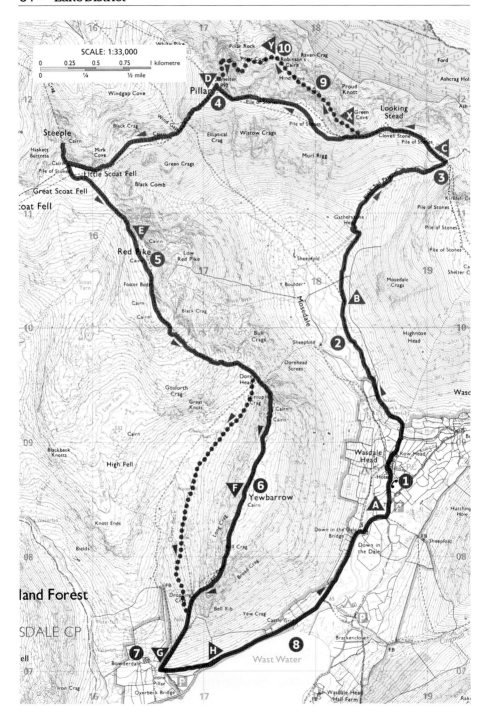

packhorse bridge. At the foot of Kirk Fell, the beck turns left among trees while the Moses' Trod path to Sty Head turns right. The Black Sail path we want climbs straight ahead between walls to the open fellsides, then follows the wall on the left northwestwards into Mosedale.

The grassy path cuts its way through thick bracken, climbing above Ritson's Force waterfalls, then descends a little into the valley-bottom fields of Mosedale.

② Mosedale NY183093
While the cliffs and screes of Yewbarrow and Red Pike on the left look impressive, Pillar looks rather like a lump, with neither a shapely outline nor severe crags to quicken the pulse.

▶ The path gradually climbs fellsides to the right of Mosedale Beck. Ignore the little path that cuts off left back towards the beck.

Approaching Pillar Rock on the more challenging alternative route to Pillar (see page 89)

After the crossing of a side stream, Gatherstone Beck, the going gets steeper and the path winds uphill to Gatherstone Head. Here, it arcs right to follow a course parallel to and high above the beck. You can either cut a corner (left) by a small cairn on a narrow path towards Looking Stead, or continue on the main path to Black Sail Pass.

③ Black Sail Pass NY192115
From the pass you look down into the head of Ennerdale where plantations of spruce and larch, first planted in the 1920s, have recently been clear-felled. More natural broadleafs will soon grow here instead. Wainwright reminisces about the time when 'the valley was open to the sky and bare of trees, and when the only sounds were the music of the beautiful river and the croaking of frogs in the mosses'.

Far below, one of England's most remote youth hostels, the Black Sail hut, lies on the fringe of the former plantations beneath Haystacks. It has only recently been supplied with electricity, by way of a small wind turbine.

▶ Turn left and climb with the path over the left shoulder of Looking Stead. Beyond this little peak follow the path along the northern edge of the fells, with fine views down Pillar's rocky coves. A line of old iron fence posts is an aid if the weather closes in.

Just beyond the next saddle, at a cairn, there is a choice of routes. The narrow path on the right is the High-level traverse path to Pillar Rock and will be described as an alternative at the end of the route.

The main route continues the climb along the edge to Pillar's summit.

④ Pillar NY172122

Pillar is an uninspiring place at first sight, with rusty iron fence posts, a stone-built trig point and two wind shelters being the only features of its stone-studded plateau.

Move to the northern wind shelter and it is a different scenario, for you look over the top of Pillar Rock's High Man, a spectacular steeple of crag. Beyond it Ennerdale Water stretches towards the Cumbrian coast.

▶ From the trig point a cairned route descends southwest to Wind Gap, an aptly named col at the head of Mosedale. It then climbs out again to Black Crag, a pleasing little summit with a good view back to Pillar.

It's Scoat Fell next. The path to it is a straightforward plod. At the summit it comes to a ridge wall on the left and follows it to a left-hand corner. From here a cairned path descends to the right (north) then climbs to a magnificent rocky perch on a rock peak well named as Steeple.

Reluctantly you retrace your steps to Scoat Fell's summit, then descend the southeast ridge with Mosedale's Red Pike ahead and Scoat Tarn in its deep grassy hollow to the right.

Climbing Pillar from the west

Red Pike

⑤ **Red Pike NY165106**
Red Pike is an angular peak with just a hint of red in its screes and precipitous crag-bound slopes plunging into Mosedale.

E▶ The path climbs among boulder and grass and passes to the right of the summit cairn, but it's an easy and quick detour to get there. Return to the path, which itself returns to the Mosedale edge, descending among outcrops of rocks to Dore Head, a deep-set pass beneath the crags of Yewbarrow. (For an easier escape route here, turn down right on the path descending to left of Over Beck).

The path clambers up the rocks of Yewbarrow's north end, Stirrup Crag, in exhilarating fashion to deposit you on a fine ridge.

⑥ **Yewbarrow NY174085**
From here you get one of the Lake District's classic views, where its leading hills parade themselves round Wasdale Head like prima donnas at an opening night party. Kirk Fell nudges in front of Great Gable across Mosedale while, across the head of Wastwater, Scafell shows its best side, easily outstripping its neighbours, Lingmell and Scafell Pike. Looking further down the lakeshores, the Wastwater Screes of Illgill Head play a supporting role.

F▶ The path continues along the ridge where rocky outcrops are surrounded by grass and bilberry. Beyond the higher south top it begins a descent to Great Door, a deep cleft in the crags with scree slopes below, plunging into the depths of Wasdale. Here the rocks of Bell Rib are too steep for walkers, and the path first turns right down scree slopes, then swings left to join a path that has come from the right from Dore

The Scafells from Yewbarrow

Head. The path descends south to a ladder stile in a wall. Once over it, follow the wall down the nose of the fell on a wide grassy path, bordered by bracken.

⑦ Joss Naylor

Champion fell-runner Joss Naylor for many years tended his Herdwick sheep in the fields of Bowderdale, beneath Yewbarrow. In the 1960s and 1970s Joss was to break record after record, including, in June 1973, the 27-mile Welsh Three-thousands in 4 hours 46 minutes. He won the Lakeland Mountain Trial ten times and extended Bob Graham's 24 hour Lakeland Record to 72 tops – a feat that won him an MBE.

The fact that Joss was a fell-runner at all was incredible, for he had previously retired from Cumberland wrestling with two suspect knees and two discs missing from his back, following surgery. Now well into his seventies, Joss can still be seen darting over the felltops.

G▶ On meeting a fence above Bowderdale Farm, the path doubles back left through the bracken to meet the narrow tarmac lane by the shores of Wastwater.

⑧ Wastwater NY174069

Across the 262ft- (80m-) deep lake the fans of Wastwater Screes dominate the landscape. Very little grows on the screes, for they frequently avalanche, destroying anything that has been trying to get a hold, including the little shoreline path. Frequent visitors to the lake include the red-breasted merganser, a sawbill duck whose head has a ragged crest, and black-headed gulls.

H▶ Turn left along the lane and follow it back to the car park.

9 The Pillar Rock High-level Path NY178121

This alternative route from Looking Stead to Pillar mountain takes the walker into spectacular crag scenery without having to resort to scrambling. It does, however, require a head for heights.

X▶ Where the ridge west of Looking Stead steepens and becomes rocky, climb just 22yds (20m) to a cairn, where you turn off right, to a narrow path traversing steep and somewhat craggy slopes above Green Cove. This is the famous Pillar High-Level Path. The devious little path has its ups and downs to avoid crags and buttresses above and below. On reaching Robinson's Cairn, Pillar Rock suddenly comes into view, a gigantic tower rising 500ft (150m) out of Pillar Cove.

High-level path to Pillar

10 Robinson's Cairn NY177124

The cairn commemorating John Wilson Robinson, who devised this splendid route, was built by friends of the climber during a storm on Easter Saturday 1908. Robinson, a farmer from Lorton, climbed the Rock one hundred and one times, though the first ascent was made by local shepherd John Atkinson in 1826.

Y▶ Cross the floor of the grassy combe beyond, and turn left up a gentle rock rib. Now the rock buttress of the Shamrock is on the right. A scree path runs up to the left of it. At the top of the scree turn right, along the top of the buttress, on a rock shelf below overhangs. This is the Shamrock Traverse, which slants up to reach a scree amphitheatre directly opposite the Rock itself. Circle the top of the amphitheatre to reach the col between the Rock and the main mountain.

The slope of the mountain, behind the col, may be ascended on rough path or by scrambling straight up slightly loose rock.

DISTANCE/ASCENT:
5 miles (8.5km) / 2,300ft
(700m)

APPROXIMATE TIME:
5 hours

HIGHEST POINT:
Great Gable summit
2,949ft (899m)

MAP:
OS Explorer OL4;
OS Landranger 89 or 90;
Harveys Lakeland West

REFRESHMENTS:
Cafés and inns at Buttermere
village and Rosthwaite;
Langstrath Inn at Stonethwaite

ADVICE:
The final ascent of Great Gable
is stony and rocky. Navigating
off Gable summit plateau is
tricky even in clear conditions

Steep-sided and high, the bowler hat shape of Gable is recognisable from almost any other summit. The high sides suggest a toilsome ascent. From Honister, however, there is a route up Great Gable that starts high and undulates. And there is a way back that wanders round the side, and views the cliff scenery from underneath.

1 Honister Pass NY226135
See Walk 14.

A From the uphill end of the car park, a path heads steeply uphill to left of the mine buildings. The newly-built pitched path makes the climb fairly easy. The path ends at a stile 220yds (200m) short of Grey Knotts' summit. But where is that summit, among the knolls and tiny pools?

When you've had enough of looking for it, head southwest along the remains of an iron fence to the cairn on Brandreth. The fence remnant continues to the tarns at Gillercomb Head, and now a wide path with cairns leads up onto Green Gable.

Eroded zigzags lead down into Windy Gap. This is a fine pass, with steep nasty-looking screes descending on both sides and crags ahead. The path up Great Gable keeps to left of the crag, but it is steep, with short steps up bare rock. As the ground eases, the path crosses boulders and stones, with many cairns, to the summit outcrop.

Great Gable and Green Gable from Styhead Tarn

Green Gable summit cairn with
Gable Crag

❷ Great Gable Summit NY211104

Gable's top, when you finally get there, is barely worth it. It's a wide plateau of rocks – and because it's so wide, and high, there almost isn't any view at all.

And yet Great Gable remains one of the most frequently trodden spots in all Cumbria. It's even popular with the dead – the fell-runner Joss Naylor has complained in print about the number of people who have their ashes scattered here, and the consequent bony grit in his trainers.

Attached to the summit rocks is the Fell & Rock Club's brass plate, a relief map of central Lakeland. The actual memorial consists of the mountains themselves: Great Gable, the Scafells, and surrounding hills. These were purchased in memory of Lakeland climbers who died in the two World Wars. A service is held on the summit of Great Gable on Commemoration Day every November.

B▶ Although the plateau of Gable hides much of the surrounding ground, there is a truly superb viewpoint just 160yds (150m) to the southwest.

❸ Westmoreland's Cairn NY210103

For every hundred on the summit, only half a dozen eat their sandwiches around Westmoreland's Cairn. But from Westmoreland's Cairn, there is a view down onto the sweeping red screes of Great Hell Gate and the spiky ridges that top off the Nape's Buttress almost directly below: then out along the length of Wasdale to the sea. The fields of Wasdale Head, their layout unchanged since the Middle Ages and possibly even prehistoric, are peculiarly satisfying. I sometimes wonder if the whole of human sheep farming

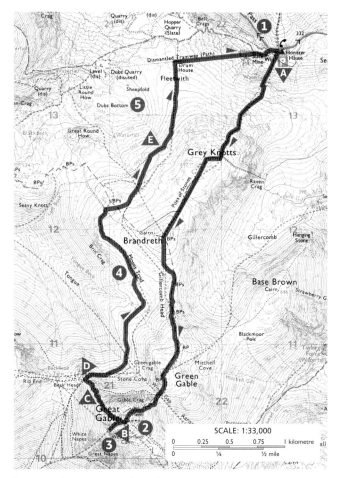

has not been directed and controlled by some off-planet intelligence simply in order to make the pattern of field walls seen from here.

C► Return to the summit. Even when it isn't misty, it's difficult to find paths off Great Gable. The stones do not show footprints, the curve of the hill hides the ridges, and in any direction you look there is a cairn. To find the path for Beck Head, head directly away from the memorial plaque – the direction is northwest. At the edge of the plateau the path becomes visible. It's an awkward descent, on bare rock, then jammed stones, then scree.

It isn't necessary to descend all the way to the col: 150ft (50m) vertically above Beckhead, the main path turns left to

slant down to that col, but our path turns down right onto the wide north face of the mountain.

Westmoreland's Cairn to Wasdale

④ Moses Trod NY212116

The path was also called 'Moses Sledgate', and was used for hauling slate from Honister around the mountain and down into Wasdale for the port at Ravenglass. However, Moses was a smuggler, with an illegal whisky still in a cave on the southern side of Great Gable. The smugglers chose their route cleverly. Starting in Wasdale, the path ends ambiguously in either Borrowdale or Buttermere; but is observed only by watchers in Ennerdale.

▷ The Moses Trod path descends at first before traversing the wide north slopes of Gable. The path passes like a whisper in the night below the crags and screes of Gable, and then of Green Gable. Hill walkers may choose to cross the boulders of Gable's summit but smugglers have more sense.

The path approaches the tarns at Gillercomb Head, passed on the outward journey. But to reach the tarns would be uphill, so instead the path bears away left, contouring around the slope of Brandreth.

⑤ Dubs Bottom NY214131

On warm sunny days in late June and into July, the mountain ringlet butterfly flutters across these grassy slopes between Grey Knotts and Dubs Bottom. This is England's one truly mountain butterfly, and is found only in the Lake District

Wasdale from high on Gable

above the 1,300ft (400m) contour – it was discovered near Ambleside in 1809.

The insect will not be seen unless the sun is shining. As soon as a cloud comes across it dives into the grass. The necessary food plant for the larvae is *Nardus stricta*, a grass that's common on all Lakeland mountains. However, the mountain ringlet has only been seen on the central fells, and not on the Skiddaw Slate of the north. Two possible reasons have been suggested. It is possible that the butterflies rely on the pockets of calcium-rich soil that occur among the Borrowdale Volcanic. Or maybe they became extinct in the north due to a difference in vegetation in the distant past, and have failed to recolonise across the deep Keswick valley. Either way, it's puzzling that the ringlet has never been recorded on the Dodds range north of Helvellyn.

The County Recorder (c/o Tullie House Museum, Carlisle CA3 8TP) will be interested in any sightings. Give date, time, weather, numbers seen and grid reference if possible.

E The Moses Trod path bends gradually left, and descends with large cairns to the highest point of the disused tramway. This was a sort of railway, powered by winch and cable, used to haul slate from the Dubs Quarry to Honister Pass.

Mount the embankment onto the tramway path, and head down it to the right. As the slope steepens, an erosion control path heads off to the left, rejoining the tramway just above the Honister quarry buildings. A stone cairn here is collecting cash for the Cockermouth Mountain Rescue Team. Heed well its mute appeal! The right of way passes out left onto the road for a few steps to reach the youth hostel and the car park.

Honister sunset at walk's end

Borrowdale

It has been suggested that Borrowdale should be pedestrianised, with a park-and-ride at Keswick. Though the idea was resisted by valley residents, we adopt it for this walk. The useful Honister Rambler bus takes us up to the Honister Pass, so that the 9 miles (14km) are walked entirely downhill. And if after the first 5 miles (8km) there should be too little time or too much tiredness, the walk around the edge of Derwentwater can be replaced by the lake ferry down its middle.

1 Honister Pass NY226135

Honister may not be the fiercest of the Lakeland passes, but it is the fiercest looking. An engraving of 1832 shows the place infested with bandits. Before setting off eastwards into Borrowdale, take a few steps westwards to look down towards Buttermere. High crags hem in the valley on both sides, with just a peep of green country and water at the bottom. The scene is rendered grimmer by debris or the slate quarries and mines.

The miners who worked these quarries in the seventeenth and eighteenth centuries were a race apart, living in hand-built shacks, commuting to work at the rock-climbing grade of Moderate and considered as savages by the valley-dwellers below. Before the building of the tramway, slate was lowered down the steep valley sides, at high speed, on crude wooden sleds. Incidentally, the Honister slates, tough and greenish-purple in colour, are rocks of the Borrowdale Volcanic, quite unrelated to the friable Skiddaw Slates of the northern fells.

A The first part of the old Honister road starts behind the youth hostel. It is used by modern quarry traffic, so walkers should be alert for the first ¼ mile (400m) down to the motor road. Head down this briefly until the old road, a damp path, forks off on the left, rejoining the road for 160yds (150m) then forking off left again as a stony track, with a bridleway sign.

2 Old Honister Road NY243143

The first 2 miles (3km) of the walk will offer wonderful views of Borrowdale with its steep, wooded sides and its flat valley floor. The flat floor is, as Wordsworth realised, a former lake bed. After the retreat of the glaciers, five lakes lay in Borrowdale. They drained away when the river finally

START:
Honister Pass (NY226135) after bus journey (Honister Rambler) from Keswick

FINISH:
Keswick. Parking in Keswick is plentiful, if expensive. There is a long-stay car park in Otley Road: if entering from the east, when the main Bell Close car park is on your left, Otley Road is a small turn-off on the right

DISTANCE/ASCENT:
8½ miles (14km) / 500ft (150m)

APPROXIMATE TIME:
5 hours

HIGHEST POINT:
Honister Pass 1,181ft (360m)

MAP:
OS Explorer OL4;
OS Landranger 89 or 90;
Harveys Lakeland West

REFRESHMENTS:
Café at Grange. Café and shop at Portinscale. Keswick has everything

ADVICE:
For bus information call 0871 200 2233. To check boat times call 017687 72263

broke through the rock bar at the Jaws of Borrowdale, but occasionally make a temporary return after heavy rain.

Trees like those in Borrowdale once covered all Lakeland below the stony summits. They were chopped down for firewood and by charcoal-burners, and to make space for sheep; and those same sheep prevented regrowth on all but the steepest and stoniest slopes. But while Borrowdale's sides preserve the natural postglacial landscape, we have to imagine the valley floor swampy, methane-smelling, inhabited by wolf, bear and beaver, and blocked by scrubby alder wood and fallen trees.

B 110yds (100m) before a larch plantation, a path branches off left, signed 'Bridleway, Grange'. It runs through bracken to a gate, then keeps ahead with a wall on its right to pass through a small col behind High Doat. Then it contours across the fellside into the gap behind Castle Crag.

A short diversion can (and should!) be taken to the summit. Leave the track at its highest point, on a small path to left of a wall.

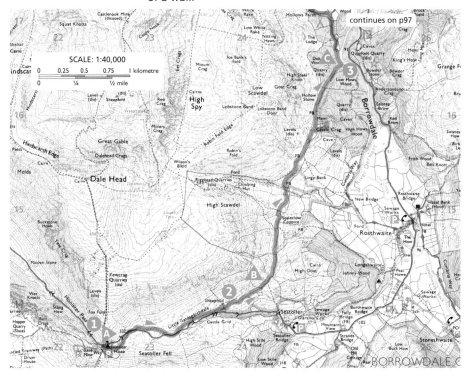

continues on p97

SCALE: 1:40,000

0   0.25   0.5   0.75   1 kilometre

0   ¼   ½ mile

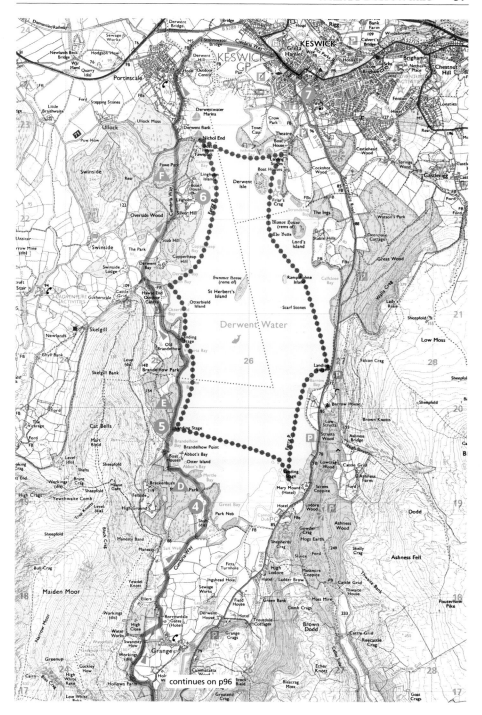

continues on p96

Upper Borrowdale, 'England's Rain Forest', with the village of Rosthwaite

The path follows a fence to two stiles, then zigzags up loose slates. On the descent, do not recross the two stiles but take a steeper path straight down to the main track.

The wide, rocky track descends through woods to reach the bank of the Derwent just upstream from Hollows camp site.

3 Jaws of Borrowdale NY251165

The name Derwent is from the British 'derwen' meaning 'oak'. The ones here are the sessile oak, which is straighter and taller than the common oak of the lowlands. There is room under the branches for flying around (if you're a bird) and catching insects. Thus the common flycatcher is found in sessile oak woods. The sessile oak has larger leaves than the common one, and its acorns have no stalks.

The oak woods of Borrowdale are referred to by the National Trust as 'England's Rain Forest'. In the shade of the trees grow various ferns, mosses and liverworts. In May the drumming of woodpeckers is virtually nonstop. The male greater spotted woodpecker is not actually after grubs, but saying to any eligible female: 'Listen: I'm really, really good at pecking wood.'

Red and roe deer live in the Borrowdale woods, though they make themselves very scarce when walkers are about.

C▷ The route continues through Hollows camp site, and then turns up left on a tarred track to pass Hollows Farm. A cart track ahead leads to High Close Wood on Peace How. Just before the wood, take a gate on the right and slant down a field to reach a road beside the Borrowdale Gates Hotel.

Turn left to a gate on the right signposted 'Footpath Lodore'. At the corner of the wood bear left slightly into the scattered trees to join the board walk. Turn left keeping the lake on the right.

4 Wheelchair Walkers NY255190

This boardwalk used to be only one person wide, leading to confrontations as to who should leap sideways into the bog, but has now been enlarged by the National Trust to wheelchair width. It will eventually be part of a complete circuit of Derwentwater. The National Park has about fifty miles of wheelchair paths. There are over twenty routes, graded for difficulty.

 ▶ The boardwalk path leads left, passing two Derwentwater bays, then reaches a track beside a house of unpainted stone.

Here turn right, leaving the trees through a gate, and passing along the lakeside and to right of a white-painted house to High Brandlehow Pier. From here a waterborne return can be taken to Keswick.

❺ Brandlehow Pier, Derwentwater NY252197
At one time this was one of the busiest industrial scenes in all Britain. In the 1550s the Company of Mines Royal was formed to exploit reserves of copper, lead, silver and gold that had been known since Roman times. Imagine ore from the Newlands valley piled at the landing stages of Derwentwater, and smoke rising from the bloomeries (smelting works) on Rampsholme Island. From the head of the lake came barges carrying Borrowdale timber to fuel the furnaces.

Brandlehow lead mine, above the pier, was still being worked in the 1850s by seventy men and boys, with a 33ft- (10m-) water wheel to drive the machinery.

 ▶ A good path continues around the lakeside to the pier at Low Brandlehow. Now the path turns slightly away from the lake, to join a track past an outdoor centre to Hawse End. At a track T-junction, with Hawse End pier down right, keep ahead and take the kissing gate on the right immediately after a track crossroads. This reaches the main entrance to Lingholm.

Looking across the head of Derwentwater into Borrowdale, with Maiden Moor behind

Looking back up Derwentwater from the foot of the lake. Catbells is behind

6 Lingholm NY252223

Beatrix Potter's Squirrel Nutkin lived in these woods, and rafted out to St Herbert's Island to gather nuts and taunt the wise old owl with simple riddles. According to Potter, Nutkin in person, tailless and irritable, may throw twigs at you from above; but I have never been assaulted in this way myself.

Nutkin is a red squirrel. Grey squirrels have reached Lakeland but are being discouraged. The reds do better than the greys in artificial plantations and conifers.

▶ 55yds (50m) after the gates of Lingholm, a path forks off left away from the boundary wall and passes under rhododendrons to the edge of Portinscale. Where the road bends left in the village, take a lane on the right to a footbridge that dangles over the River Derwent. After 220yds (200m) a path runs to the right, into the edge of Keswick. If you head straight into the town you reach the Moot Hall.

7 Moot Hall NY266234

This is now an information centre, but was formerly a courthouse and prison. The iron door of the cell now opens onto piles of leaflets. But the building is still associated with human suffering: it's the start and finish point of the Bob Graham twenty-four hour run over forty-two Lakeland summits, and also of the 43 mile- (70km-) walk around the four 3,000ft- (915m-) mountains.

Ullscarf & Watendlath from Rosthwaite

Though Ullscarf is not the most popular of Lakeland's fells, to walk it from Rosthwaite is a real pleasure. New scenes unfold with each turn: the Stonethwaite Valley and the buttress of Eagle Crag; the wild windswept Ullscarf plateau; Walpole's Watendlath and its pretty tarn; then the finale, Borrowdale's beautiful green valley threading through some of England's highest mountains.

1 Rosthwaite NY257148

Rosthwaite, which means clearing on a heap of stones, was built by the sides of the How, a rocky knoll overlooking the fields of Borrowdale. During the last ice age there would have been a huge lake here, one of four, in the upper valley. As the glaciers retreated, the lakes were gradually filled up with debris carried down by mountain streams.

A Turn left out of the car park and follow the lane to the main Borrowdale road in the village. Turn left for a few yards, then right on a footpath that crosses the bridge over Stonethwaite Beck. The route will follow Wainwright's *Coast to Coast* walk up to Greenup Edge.

Turn right to follow a stony bridleway by the beck's east (left) bank. Soon the bridleway leaves the main valley, veering left towards Stonethwaite. The village and its little camp site lie across the beck and there's a bridge for those who want to detour to see the place.

START/FINISH:
National Trust car park at Rosthwaite, Borrowdale (NY257148)

DISTANCE/ASCENT:
10 miles (16km) / 2,300ft (700m)

APPROXIMATE TIME:
6½ hours

HIGHEST POINT:
Ullscarf summit 2,382ft (726m)

MAP:
OS Explorer OL4;
OS Landranger 90;
Harveys Lakeland Central

REFRESHMENTS:
Watendlath café;
Rosthwaite has a café and inns

ADVICE:
The tops from Greenup Edge to Long Moss can be very boggy, especially outside the summer months. Save this one for July or August or try it on a clear, crisp, frosty day

Eagle Crag and Stonethwaite Beck

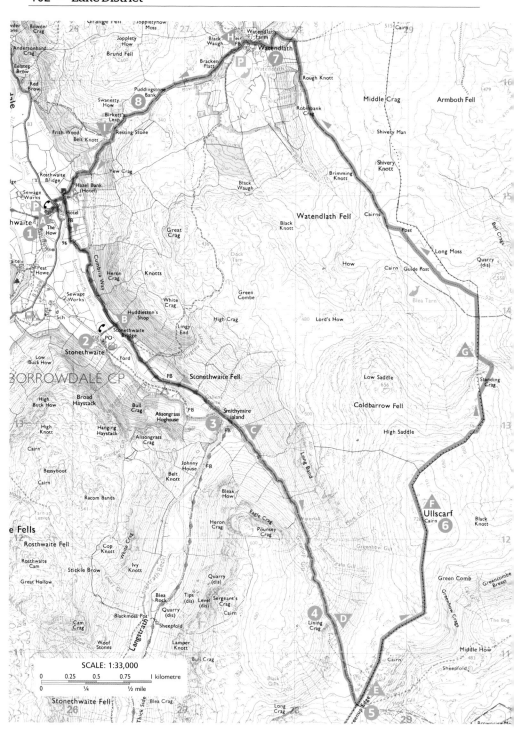

Ullscarf, seen across Blea Tarn

② Stonethwaite NY263137

Though Borrowdale was owned by the monks of Furness Abbey, the old Norse settlement of Stonethwaite belonged to Fountains Abbey in Yorkshire. There is a cluster of whitewashed cottages and the little church of St Andrew which was first consecrated in 1687.

In the churchyard lies the grave of Bob Graham, a mountain man of these parts who devised the Bob Graham Round to celebrate his forty-second birthday. The round consisted of forty-two peaks and 26,000ft (8,000m) of ascent, which Graham completed in twenty-three hours.

B▸ Beyond Stonethwaite follow the beck beneath High Crag on your left, with the impressive Eagle Crag towering ahead on your right above the bouldery beck. Continue along the bridleway through several gates and past Gallery Force (waterfall).

③ Smithymire Island NY274130

At Smithymire Island, between the Langstrath and Stonethwaite becks, the monks of Furness Abbey used to smelt iron ore. This would have been mined from the mountainsides at Ore Gap and transported by packhorse trains down Langstrath.

C▸ As you gain height you can see that Eagle Crag and Heron Crag separate the Stonethwaite valley into two valleys: that of Langstrath, which branches to the right, and Greenup Gill.

This route stays with the beck to the left, which has now become Greenup Gill. The valley becomes more austere and treeless. The path continues to climb up alongside the beck, passing some fine waterfalls on the way to Lining Crag, a prominent landmark on the skyline.

④ Lining Crag NY283113

Beneath the crag you will see a series of grassy, whalebacked mounds. Known as drumlins, these are formed from the moraine debris from a glacier. You should also see starry saxifrage (*Saxifraga stellaris*). This little plant with low toothed leaves, long stem and small white flowers, revels in these moist acid soils and the shade of the surrounding rocks.

D▶ Bear left towards the front of Lining Crag and pick up the stone path. Immediately ahead the route becomes a bit of a scramble over rocks until the path emerges again to lead up and behind the crag. The odd cairn shows the way. From the top of the crag the terrain becomes a little marshy, a theme that will largely persist until the descent to Watendlath. A peaty path, reminiscent of the Pennines, heads south-southeast to reach the col of Greenup Edge.

⑤ Greenup Edge NY286105

Greenup Edge, a wild pass between High Raise and Ullscarf, has several shallow pools which are filled with bogbean (*Menyanthes trifoliata*). This attractive if common aquatic plant has pale pink flowers that appear between April and June.

E▶ From Greenup Edge, the route leaves the *Coast to Coast* walk and turns left for Ullscarf, following a scant line of old iron fence posts, and climbing past more pools and rocky outcrops to the summit.

⑥ Ullscarf NY292123

Ullscarf, which means the wolf's pass, isn't the finest summit in Lakeland: the wolves have long gone, it's wet, it's windswept, and it's only got a small cairn. However, Ullscarf is the centre of Lakeland, and, as such, it offers good views of the other peaks. Beyond its wide convex upper slopes, you can see the Helvellyn group, the Scafells and Great Gable beyond Langstrath, Windermere on the southern horizon, and Skiddaw and Blencathra to the north.

F▶ From the summit, the route heads north until it comes to the corner of a post and wire stock fence. Here, bear to the right and follow the fence northeastwards with Helvellyn in view ahead and fleeting glimpses of Blea Tarn to the left.

The route comes to an abrupt halt at Standing Crag, where it detours to the right to descend steep, grassy flanks.

 The fence-side path resumes at the bottom, and Blea Tarn comes back into view. Ignore the first gate in the fence (the bridleway – pathless), but go through the second, where a very sketchy route now leads across damp heather-scattered moorland of Long Moss on the northeast (right hand) side of the tarn.

By the far end of the tarn a notice points out a route avoiding Bleatarn Gill. Follow this course, climbing NNW across the slopes of Brimming Knott. The path gets a little lost in the moor grasses in places and this could be confusing in mist.

Watendlath Tarn comes into view, and the path comes down to the intake wall at the edge of the moorland. Beyond a wall corner the path turns left and descends towards Watendlath. The last zigzags have been heavily engineered by the National Trust, using local stone.

Beyond a gate, the path joins an enclosed, unsurfaced lane. (NB: The stile to the left leads to the Watendlath car park and toilets beyond which there is a café.) The lane in turn leads to the tarmac road from Derwent Water.

Watendlath Bridge

Eagle Crag above the waterfalls
of Greenup Gill

7 Watendlath NY276164

Hugh Walpole described Watendlath as 'the heart of Lake Country, and therefore, the heart of England'. He made it the setting for the second of his Herries Chronicles, *Judith Paris*. Fold Head Farm is generally believed to be Judith Paris's house. It has a view of the tarn from the front door, two storeys and an inside staircase. In the story Judith's ne'er-do-well husband Georges is killed by being thrown down the stairs. His murderer was the father of a man Georges himself had murdered by drowning in a small boat at Bergen harbour on the way to a house of ill repute.

Watendlath was linked to Rosthwaite, Wythburn and Ashness by packhorse trails. There is a packhorse bridge at the north end of Watendlath Tarn, which is crammed with water lilies and tall club rushes. You may see swifts fluttering overhead. By the sides of the stream pied and grey wagtails can be seen in their characteristic jerky flight. Also present in spring and early summer is the common sandpiper, a wading bird with brown wings and a white breast.

H▶ Cross the packhorse bridge and take the path to the left, then turn up the right fork, a stony bridleway climbing above woodland and beneath the rocky knoll of Bracken Platt. It reaches its highest point at Puddingstone Bank, and from here the views of Borrowdale become ever more rewarding with each step.

8 Puddingstone Bank and the Cuckoo of Borrowdale NY266157

From this lofty position on a quiet spring evening you will probably be able to hear the cuckoo calling down in the woods of Borrowdale, though it is quite elusive in flight. The cuckoo looks a bit like a small hawk in flight, but its wing beats are more rapid and urgent.

A legend exists that the inhabitants of Borrowdale tried to prevent the cuckoo from leaving by building a wall across the bottom of the valley. Their reasoning was that when the cuckoo leaves, summer ends, bringing on the onset of winter.

I▶ The stony path descends past the conifers on Birkett's Leap, before veering left. Beneath Yew Crag, go right through a farm gate to join the outward route by the bridge over Stonethwaite Beck. Cross the bridge, turn left along the Borrowdale road, then right along the road to return to the car park at Rosthwaite.

Walla Crag & Derwentwater

This easy walk on the crags above Keswick and Derwentwater is one of the most spectacular. If you do it in August or early September the heather will be at its best and Walla Crag will be a colourful platform for some of the finest views Lakeland can offer.

1 Great Wood NY274217

Great Wood would once have been filled with native broadleaved trees such as oaks. Hazel, rowans and ash still thrive here, though now they are outnumbered by plantations of larch.

The wood is currently under the ownership of the National Trust, who bought the land after a charitable appeal was set up in 1920 to celebrate the life of founder member, Canon Hardwicke Rawnsley. Rawnsley, an early advocate of increased public access to beautiful scenery, lived in Crosthwaite, near Kendal.

The netted carpet moth, a rare species, colonises the wood. These moths will only lay their eggs on touch-me-not, a variety of balsam found here. The adult moth can be seen in flight during August.

In a report of 1759, it was claimed that Cat Gill, which will be crossed early in the day, was a stronghold of wildcats 'of the tyger kind', and that during Whitsun tide 12 had been killed (wildcats, not people!).

START/FINISH:
Car park at Great Wood, Derwentwater (NY271214)

DISTANCE/ASCENT:
6 miles (10km) / 1,000ft (320m)

APPROXIMATE TIME:
4 hours

HIGHEST POINT:
Walla Crag 1,243ft (379m)

MAP:
OS Explorer OL4;
OS Landranger 90;
Harveys Lakeland Central

REFRESHMENTS:
Kiosk by ferry landing stages at Keswick

ADVICE:
Do this walk in August when the heather will be blooming on the summit of Walla Crag

On Walla Crag summit looking to Blencathra

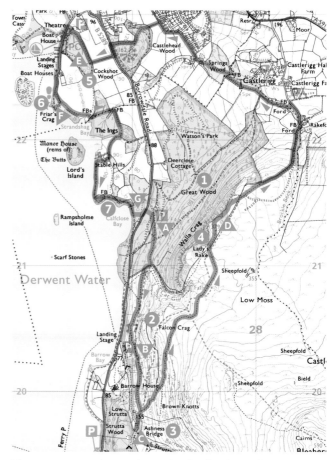

The creature was hunted to extinction by the early nineteenth century.

A Just above the car park's one-way exit road, take a signposted public footpath gently uphill (south). Past a vehicle barrier, ignore the wider stony path which goes steeply uphill on the left. On the approach to Cat Gill the path has been laid with cobbles. Leave it here for a permissive lower route on the right, which first crosses a footbridge over Cat Gill before heading south by a wall and beneath magnificent oaks. It soon emerges on the bracken-cloaked slopes, with scabious and harebells growing on grass patches between the rocks. The undulating path continues high above the shore of Derwentwater and beneath the rocks and screes of Falcon Crag. On reaching a cairn take the left hand path sign posted 'Ashness Bridge'.

Brockle Beck above
Derwentwater

② Falcon Crag NY273203
Peregrine falcons can still be seen soaring in the skies above. Further down the valley, you may see climbers grappling with a 150ft- (50m-) rock face on Lower Falcon Crag.

▶ The path crosses several small streams and eventually reaches a gate where Ashness Bridge is in sight. Go through the gate and down to Ashness Bridge.

③ Ashness Bridge NY271196
This typical one-arched packhorse bridge is probably the most photographed in Lakeland – certainly the view across it towards Skiddaw is a splendid one. This old traders' route climbed to Watendlath then over the fells to Armboth.

▶ Retrace your steps and go through the last-mentioned gate, but this time take the upper right fork, which climbs up the higher craggy slopes. There is a very short scrambly section before the path resumes through more bracken to cross a stile in a wire fence and climb the hillside above Falcon Crag.

Eventually the path rounds the head of Cat Gill, and now you see some heather. This heather provides the ideal habitat for the northern eggar and emperor moths. To the right, beyond heather and grass, bare moorland slopes rise to Bleaberry Fell.

The common butterwort grows in the marshy places hereabouts. It has a blue flower and pale green leaves with curled-up edges whose sappy surface catches small insects.

Go over the stile in a wall gap, which gives access to the rock and heather top of Walla Crag.

Friar's Crag, Derwentwater

4 Walla Crag NY277214

Windswept larch, rowan and birch are scattered among the rocks at the top of the crag. Skiddaw's smooth, swooping slopes of scree and heather can be seen beyond Derwentwater and the buildings of Keswick, while the colourful heather and bracken hills of Newlands and Grasmoor fill the western horizon. To the northeast, beyond the green fields of Threlkeld, Blencathra completes the picture.

The great ravine that rends the crags is known as Lady's Rake. It is named after Lady Radcliffe, wife of Sir Francis Radcliffe, the Earl of Derwentwater, who was executed for treason after the Jacobite rebellion of 1715. While the parliamentary forces were attacking the family mansion on Lord's Island on Derwentwater, Lady Radcliffe collected all the valuables she could and fled. It must have been an arduous route up Walla Crag, but the story is corroborated by the discovery of gold coins between the rocks.

▶ Follow a path northeast along the cliff edge, then through the heather to a gate. Go through this down a wide grassy slope between bracken. Keep the wall on your left as the path rises and then descends into the small valley of Brockle Beck. Here the path bends left to follow the stream, goes through a gate then crosses the stream on a footbridge in the shade of some trees.

The track turns left to meet the end of a tarmac lane at Rakefoot Farm. Follow the lane northwards. For berry collectors or wine makers the hedgerows and thickets are full of raspberries, blackberries, elder and wild rose.

After 330yds (300m) turn sharp left then right through a gate signposted 'Keswick, Great Wood'. The path recrosses Brockle Beck on a footbridge, then turns right, parallel to the stream and along the top edge of Springs Wood, by a waymarked path.

Go through a gate, pass to the right of a radio mast and continue down a stony path which turns right into the wood. Do not cross the footbridge over the beck, but turn left, tracing the beck's west banks.

The path emerges from the trees, passes through a gate and goes to the right of Springs Farm onto a lane. Follow the lane, Springs Road, for about $1/3$ mile (500m) before turning left on a narrow path, bound by a hedge on one side and a wire fence on the other, which heads west to Castlehead Wood.

Beyond a gate, the path enters the wood. Follow the widest path, which climbs towards the top of the hill. When it reaches the top corner of a field, leave this path for one on the right, which follows the perimeter westwards to Borrowdale Road. A short detour to the top of Castlehead, which is another good viewpoint, can be made by keeping to the path continuing uphill at the field corner.

Turn left along a path just beyond the road. Now it is almost a repeat performance as a narrow path bound by a hedge on one side and a wire fence on the other, heads west across a field into Cockshot Wood.

⑤ Cockshott Wood NY265227
Cockshot is a corruption of cock-shut, ie. twilight. Among its trees are oak, hazel, sycamore, beech and ash. Wood anemones and dog's mercury flourish here, as do garlic and bluebells. On the path up to the wood you may see orange-tipped butterflies, who favour the local hedge garlic.

 Once in the wood, turn right and follow the wide path to the Lakeside car park near the Keswick landing stages.

Turn left out of the car park, and left again just past the Theatre by the Lake to the landing stages. It's usually a busy place where ducks demand to be fed and ice creams demand to be eaten. A tarmac lane runs parallel to the shores of Derwentwater. It later becomes a gravel path, rounding the headland above Friar's Crag. Bear left past Ruskin's Stone. The path goes down to a gate and on to the grassland and stony shore.

⑥ Friar's Crag NY264223
The low dolerite crag overlooks the lake and the small wooded Derwent and Lord's Islands. Victorian writer and philosopher

Ruskin's Memorial, Friar's Crag

Looking across Derwentwater to Causey Pike and the Grasmoor group of fells

Descent to Brockle Beck, with Blencathra in the background

John Ruskin rated the view from here as one of the three most beautiful in Europe. His earliest memories were of being brought here as a five year old by his nurse. The National Trust has erected a small memorial to him above the crag.

F Go round the shore to Strandshag Bay, then into the marshy woodlands of the Ings, a Site of Special Scientific Interest. Keep to the main path here, which heads inland passing through wetlands that include water mint, yellow flag iris, meadowsweet and branched burweed, then turns right over a footbridge. Stream outwash here records the severe floods of winter 2009. Continue to a gate at the woodland edge, and turn right along a surfaced track that passes Stable Hills Farm, owned by the National Trust. After the farm a path veers left to trace the lakeshore opposite Lord's Island. This is now also listed as a Site of Special Scientific Interest. Beyond a gate in a fence, it swings left beneath the yew trees at Broomhill Point.

Ashness Bridge

⑦ The Centenary Sculpture NY266215

On the gravel beach lies the Centenary Sculpture. Known as the Hundred Year Stone, this was sculpted by Peter Randall Page from a split glacial Borrowdale boulder. It is dedicated to the first 100 years of the National Trust and all the people who helped them to acquire land – from the early pioneers like local man Canon Hardwicke Rawnsley to the twentieth-century Trust members.

G Halfway along the shores of Calfclose Bay, you come to an NT moneybox cairn. Turn back sharp left, on a path that joins the Borrowdale road opposite the entrance to Great Wood car park.

A Newlands Horseshoe

The Newlands Valley has no main roads or huge pay car parks, nor has it been subjected to much tourism. It is unspoilt, it is beautiful and it is green, with shapely hills of heather and bracken. From Little Town, where a few whitewashed cottages are clustered beneath the Cat Bells – High Spy ridge and Scope End, there is a great way to these fells. It's a horseshoe walk that takes in Robinson, Hindscarth and Dale Head, then adds High Spy and Maiden Moor for afters. A tough but very rewarding walk.

1 Little Town NY233195

Beatrix Potter visited Little Town often, and was friendly with the vicar of Newlands Church. In *The Tale of Mrs Tiggy-Winkle*, Lucie of Littletown has been modelled on the vicar's daughter, Lucie Carr. Mrs Tiggy-Winkle's cottage was on the lower slopes of Cat Bells just above the village.

A Follow the road downhill across Chapel Bridge, which spans Newlands Beck, before turning left through a gate onto the tarmac lane signposted to Newlands Church.

2 Newlands Church NY230194

Newlands Church, unusually, hasn't been dedicated to any saint. Though plain it is nevertheless attractive with its white walls shaded by sycamores. Wordsworth wrote:

> *How delicate the leafy veil*
> *Through which yon house of God*
> *Gleams mid the peace of this deep dale,*
> *By few but shepherds trod!*

Through the valley of Scope Beck with Robinson in the distance

START/FINISH:
Small car park at Little Town, Newlands Valley (NY233194), but get there early before it fills up

DISTANCE/ASCENT:
9 miles (15km) / 3,500ft (1,050m)

APPROXIMATE TIME:
7 hours

HIGHEST POINT:
Dale Head 753m (2,470ft)

MAP:
OS Explorer OL4;
OS Landranger 90;
Harveys Lakeland Central

REFRESHMENTS:
Nearest are at Swinside Inn 1 mile (2km) north along Portinscale road

ADVICE:
The climb from the unnamed tarn at High Crags to the summit of Robinson is steep in places and serious in wintry conditions. Several escape routes lead back to the car park: from Littledale Edge, head north keeping up to left of Scope Beck to the outward route by the unnamed tarn. From the col between Hindscarth and Dale Head (NY214157) descend alongside Near Tongue Gill. This joins the right-of-way path from the summit to Newlands Beck. Both routes are pathless but safe

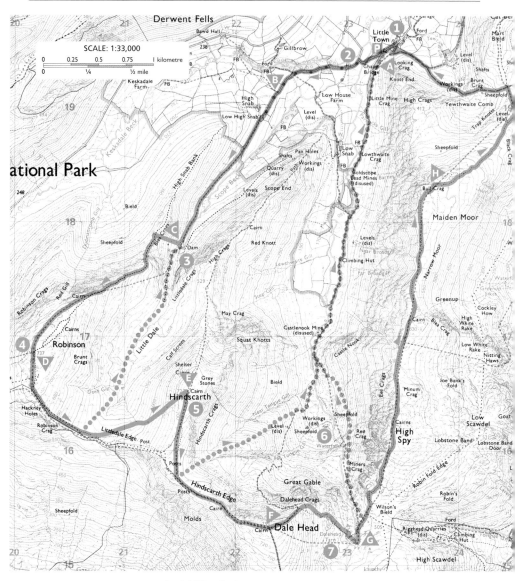

In 1877 a little schoolhouse was added, but this was closed in 1967. Look out for the memorial stone to Dorothy Potts, who was the schoolmistress between 1943 and 1966.

B The lane continues up the valley of Scope Beck. It passes beneath the imposing whitewashed farmhouse of High Snab before coming to an end at the more rustic Low High Snab Cottage.

The route continues beyond the gate as a stony track climbs in the shade of some sycamores before continuing across open fellsides. Those who want to get onto the ridge early at Scope End can climb right on a grass path through bracken. My favoured route continues along the now grassy track that delves deeper into the valley of Scope Beck.

❸ Unnamed Reservoir NY215178
A gloomy little reservoir at the head of the valley is overlooked by dark crags with rowan trees clinging to them.

▶ The old mine track leads no further than the top of the waterfalls running down the crags. Fortunately, there's a better route. A grassy rake climbs from the north head of the lake to a little tree on the skyline on the right. It's a steep but short pull to the ridge, High Snab Bank.

The climb from High Snab Bank to Robinson is a steep but memorable one, scrambling over three short rock steps to get to the top of Blea Crags – you will need to use your hands hereabouts. Higher up, the path climbs above Robinson Crags, which plunge 1,000ft (300m) into Keskadale.

A cairn marks the edge of Robinson's stony summit plateau, which has two distinct parallel outcrops of rock. The main path passes the highest point, which lies on the western outcrop, but you'll have to make a detour to the right to see the best views.

❹ Robinson NY202168
Robinson takes its name from a former landowner, Richard Robinson. The views encompass Crummock Water, the Grasmoor group of fells and Red Pike. Buttermere Moss hides much of Buttermere, but unfamiliar corners of Great Gable, Pillar and Scafell make up for it.

▶ From the summit, follow the path south across the stony plateau to a fence that guides the route of descent southeast down Littledale Edge. Note how the heather is growing on the other side of the fence, where the sheep cannot graze.

The climb to Hindscarth is a steep one. From the low point of the col, you could take the path and fence ahead to miss out Hindscarth. But our route forks left on a path that slants northeast across the slope to reach Hindscarth's summit cairn.

Dale Head from Hindscarth

5 Hindscarth NY216165

This broad hill rises up above the marshes of Little Dale and the upper Newlands Valley. Being off the main horseshoe route, it's quieter than its neighbours. Although not a spectacular summit, Hindscarth gives an excellent view to the cliffs and gullies of Dale Head and Eel Crags.

Follow the ridgeline south to a dip, and fork left on a path which slants down to the main ridge at Hindscarth Edge. The wide path climbs the steep rocky flanks of Dale Head to the tall summit cairn.

6 Dale Head and its Mines NY229160

As you stand by the cairn on Dale Head, the ground falls away beneath your feet into the depths of the upper Newlands Valley. Eel Crags, a long line of splintered cliffs and screes, guides the rugged mine-scarred valley to the softer fields of Littletown.

You can also make out crumbling buildings and spoil heaps – the remains of old mine workings – by Far Tongue Gill, at Castlenook, and further down the valley at Goldscope. These mines contained valuable ores or lead, copper, silver and a little gold.

Though some date back to the thirteenth century, most of the mines in this area were developed four centuries later by the Company of Mines Royal with the help of experienced German miners. In 1607 Daniel Hechstetter discovered veins of copper and lead at the Dale Head mine, the one by Far Tongue Gill. The name Goldscope was a corruption of Gott es gab, which is German for God's gift. This mine had two parallel veins of lead, one 14ft (4.2m) and the other 9ft (2.7m) thick. The mines had a chequered history, many closing during the Civil War, before reopening during the Industrial Revolution. By the turn of the last century they had all been closed.

From Dale Head there's a steep stony path east down to Dale Head Tarn. It's not the right-of-way shown on current OS maps, but the black dashes shown on Harvey and other maps.

The path descends northeast to a small shoulder, then turns steeply down right (southeast). In these lower reaches it has been pitched with boulders. It descends over a carpet of alpine lady's mantle to a sheepfold by the northern shores of Dale Head Tarn.

⑦ Dale Head Tarn NY230153

Dale Head Tarn lies in a shallow, marshy bowl surrounded by rushes and rocky knolls. It's tangled with pondweed and buzzing with dragonflies. I've seen both the golden ringed (yellow and black) and common hawker (blue and black) varieties. You may see rival males looping-the-loop in aerial battle, or females after mating trying to bury their eggs in the mud.

⑥ The path circumvents a rocky knoll before fording Newlands Beck, which tumbles down a rocky ravine on the left. The rocks are clad with maidenhair fern, heather and juniper. (For a more sheltered escape route here, take the path down to the right of the beck and along Newlands.)

The path climbs to the left among rocky outcrops to the tall summit cairn of High Spy. The hard work is over when you've accomplished this, for the ridge is now an easy promenade, among rocks at first, then mat grass and heather at Narrow Moor.

Here the ridge narrows and Derwentwater comes into view, as does the little village of Grange, surrounded by a patchwork of fields and wooded crags. The wide path passes below and to right of Maiden Moor's slight rise – the small branch path left gives better views.

⑥ North of Maiden Moor the marked right of way would have you leaping off crags. The true line of the path lies further east, following the black dashed path of both the

On Dale Head's summit

Return to Little Town in the Newlands Valley, with Causey Pike on the horizon

OS and Harveys maps. Again at Bull Crag take the left fork, which gives good views over the edge of Bull Crag and into the Newlands Valley. The path descends close to the Borrowdale edge to reach Hause Gate, the pass dividing Maiden Moor and Catbells.

At Hause Gate descend left on a grassy bridleway, then take the left fork, descending past mine workings. A multi-cairned, stony chute of slag takes the route down to Yewthwaite Gill.

Across the gill, the bridleway transforms into a grassy track raking left down the hillsides, with the pleasant green fields and heather-covered hills of Newlands ahead.

The track meets the Yewthwaite Mine track and a wall, both coming in from the right. The flinted track descends further above the whitewashed cottages of Little Town. At a junction, double back right to get to the road at the west end of the tiny hamlet. Turn left and descend the peaceful lane back to the car park.

High Stile

A 3km- (2 mile-) crest, rocky but almost level, links Red Pike, High Stile and High Crag. On the left it drops steeply to the Buttermere valley; on the right it drops even more steeply to Ennerdale. This is the best of ridgewalking. We get onto the ridge by way of Crummock Water side and a waterfall.

1 Buttermere NY176169

The Fish Inn at Buttermere was the site of the big scandal of 1802. The innkeeper's daughter, Mary Robinson, was already known as the 'Beauty of Buttermere'. She charmed an illustrious visitor, the Honourable Colonel Augustus Hope, Member of Parliament and brother to Lord Hopetoun. A few weeks later they were married in Buttermere Church.

The Honourable Colonel was unlucky. The poet Coleridge wrote about the romance in *The Morning Post*, and Lord Hopetoun began to wonder what his brother was doing marrying a barmaid when he was known to be away touring the Continent. The bridegroom was exposed as an impostor called James Hatfield, with several other supposed wives in various parts of England.

Even in 1802, bigamy and impostures were not capital crimes. However, the supposed MP had taken advantage of his privilege of franking his own mail and sending it free of

START/FINISH:
Buttermere (NY176170); car parks in the village, or National Trust pay-and-display 300m down the valley (NY173172). In the summer, look out for the bus service, the Honister Rambler

DISTANCE/ASCENT:
8½ miles (14km) / 2,600ft (800m)

APPROXIMATE TIME:
6½ hours

HIGHEST POINT:
High Stile summit 2,644ft (806m)

MAP:
OS Explorer OL4;
OS Landranger 89;
Harvey's Lakeland West

REFRESHMENTS:
Buttermere village has two good pubs, the Bridge and the Fish, Croft House Café, and Syke House Farm tea room for home-made ice cream

ADVICE:
From Scarth Gap you can continue on Walk 19 (Haystacks) for a combined walk of 12 miles (19km) / 3,900ft (1,200m) / 9 hours

High Crag from Buttermere, where the walk starts

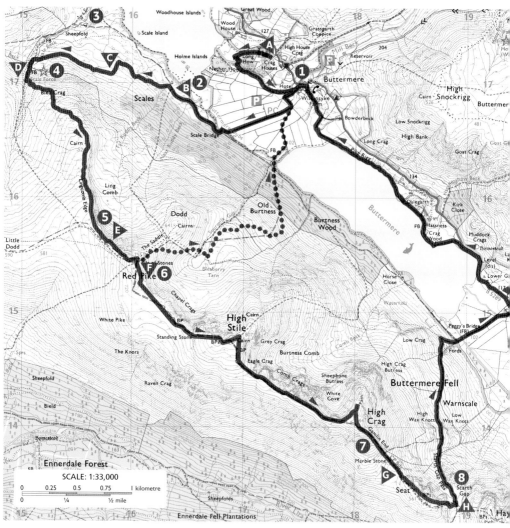

charge. He was prosecuted by the Post Office for this forgery, and hanged for it at Carlisle. Mary married a Buttermere farmer but remained a tourist attraction. Thomas de Quincey did not know what the fuss was about: 'good-looking, but *beautiful* in any sense she was not.' She has been turned into good romantic fiction by Melvyn Bragg (*The Maid of Buttermere*, 1984).

A If starting from the National Trust car park, you can leave through a gate in the northwest corner. This heads away through a wood to Sail Beck. Keep ahead for 110yds (100m) downstream, then cross a footbridge and double back along the stream side to Buttermere village.

Take the track to left of the Fish Inn, with a sign for Scale Bridge. After 220yds (200m) the path bends right; but immediately before this corner is a gate on the right onto a side track. After the bridge over Buttermere Dubs, a rough path leads to the right along the base of Red Pike's northern spur.

❷ Crummock Water Side NY165170

The path cleverly contours a metre or so above the marshy valley floor. In summer the floor is white-speckled with cotton grass and the frothy blooms of meadowsweet. A tall pink flower that can be spotted among the meadowsweet is the herb valerian.

B▶ At the end of the wood you cross a narrow footbridge. Here fork up left, on a path slanting gradually uphill around a grassy spur with thorn trees, overlooking Crummock Water.

❸ Scale Beck NY151170

There are traces of a British settlement in the flat ground at the foot of Scale Beck. The name of the place suggests that Briton was quickly displaced by Norseman on this prime lakeside site. 'Scale' is from 'skali', Norse for 'hut'.

C▶ A large cairn marks where the path turns abruptly left, uphill. After 110yds (100m) it turns back to the right. Stony and marked with cairns, the path leads round to the footbridge at the base of Scale Force.

❹ Scale Force NY150171

With a drop of 154ft (47m), this is the highest waterfall in Lakeland. It plunges into a gorge whose luxuriant birch and rowan indicate the natural cover of this hill ground in places not nibbled by sheep. The trees also obstruct the view of the waterfall. However, you win whatever the weather. In the wet, the noise and spate are impressive despite the branches in the way. In the dry, you can scramble up the small left-hand branch of the watercourse, to reach the very foot of the main fall. Water-washed rocks are clean and firm, giving a short and fairly easy climb. However, algae-coated rocks away from the stream are very slippery.

D▶ Paths lead uphill on either side of the waterfall gorge: the one on its left has been repaired and is the easier.

Scale Force. The foot of the upper fall, reached after a short scramble when the beck is low

Return a few steps along the path you arrived on, then turn uphill on the repaired zigzag path. It heads up between trees and small outcrops. As the slope eases, the path heads to the left, along the top of the steep drops to Crummock Water. The ascending ridge is broad and grassy.

⑤ Red Pike North Ridge NY158155

The occasional boulder fields on the ridge are of rough, rounded stones that show pink on exposed surfaces, though weathering to grey. This is the Ennerdale Granophyre – the gorge of Scale Force was made of this rock. As the ridge steepens to the final cone, there is a clear transition across the line where stone fields give way to orange scree. Above this line are outcrops of Borrowdale Volcanic rocks, sharpedged and grey. This rock is harder and weathers less, and breaks with sharp corners.

▶ A path zigzags up the scree, soon to reach Red Pike's summit. (To shorten the walk at this point, take the steep path down the spur northeast, then down past Bleaberry Tarn.)

⑥ Red Pike NY161154

The 2,000ft (600m) just ascended is reason for a rest, but for those who need further excuse, the summit of Red Pike is the best standpoint from which to examine the three main rocks of Lakeland.

Across the valley at the back of Ennerdale Water, rounded rolling hills are made of the Ennerdale Granophyre. (Granophyre is like granite, but finer-grained.) Soft and water soluble, this erodes into ordinary-looking hills such as Starling Dodd. The pinkish rock can be seen exposed on the face of Caw Fell, above the head of the lake.

In the opposite direction, across Buttermere, are the hills of the Grasmoor group and beyond them, Skiddaw. These elegant hills have steep, smooth sides and pointed crests. They are the Skiddaw Slate.

All around the head of Ennerdale are hills of a different sort: the lumpy, chunky mountains that we think of as the real Lakeland. Steeple, Pillar and Gable are carved from the rock the rock climbers climb on: the tough grey rock of the Borrowdale Volcanic Series. After having it easy through the granophyre, the glacier that formed Ennerdale Water had to break out through some Borrowdale Volcanic: this

Looking from Red Pike to
High Stile just after sunrise

forms the twin gateposts of Anglers' Crag (left) and Bowness Knott (right).

F A path keeps close to the steep left-hand drops as it makes its way along the ridge of rock and stones to High Stile. This summit is set a little out towards Buttermere: in mist, note that you must return southwest for 110yds (100m) to regain the main ridge line. The ridge then runs southeast to High Crag.

From High Crag a stony path descends southeast. As the slope steepens, the path becomes a pitched one that goes down in sharp zigzags.

7 Gamlin End NY182138

This whole slope was a trodden eroded scree – ugly to look at, and very unpleasant to go up or down. Gradually, human feet were transporting the entire end of High Crag down into Scarth Gap. During the summer of 1997 the National Trust's path team built this pitched path. In construction it resembles the traditional pack-pony routes of the area, though little merchandise would ever have needed to be transported over High Stile. Such paths are definitely the least bad solution to the problem of path erosion, being rugged enough to preserve the feel of the hill and blending in visually after only a couple of years. Considerate walkers will not stray off the path onto the regrown grass alongside.

G The ridge levels briefly, then makes a short climb to Seat. The path bypasses this minor summit on the left. A steep pitched path leads down into Scarth Gap.

Path passing Seat on the descent to Scarth Gap near the end of the walk

8 Scarth Gap NY189134

This was a major pass between Buttermere and Ennerdale, and is still a popular through route for walkers and cyclists. Here you may decide to transfer to Walk 19, which continues ahead over Haystacks.

H▶ The well-used path doubles back to the left (north) to slant down to the valley floor. After passing along the top of a plantation, turn back sharp right to descend the plantation's lower edge to Peggy's Bridge. Paths lead back to Buttermere village along either side of the lake. The route by Gatesgarth offers splendid views across the water to the High Stile Ridge. Also, there is often an ice-cream van at Gatesgarth.

A wide path crosses the valley floor to Gatesgarth.

I▶ Turn left along the road, using a verge footpath. Just after you reach the lake, the lakeside footpath branches off on the left. It leads through woodland, and through a 65yd- (60m-) tunnel in the rock, to the foot of Buttermere. Here the main path keeps ahead between fields to Buttermere village.

Fleetwith Pike from Buttermere

Haystacks

Haystacks may be low, but this is a full-blooded Lakeland mountain walk and never mind the altitude. There is plenty of fine rock scenery, some of which has to be walked over.

① Gatesgarth NY196150

For over a century, Gatesgarth Farm and its successive owners, the Nelsons and the Richardsons, have been famous for their Herdwick sheep. This ancient breed – possibly going back to the Britons – changes colour as it grows. The lambs are almost black, the one-year-old 'hoggs' are peaty brown, and the mature sheep almost white. Small and agile, they are supremely adapted to fell life.

'The mountain sheep are sweeter but the valley sheep are fatter' – and the Herdwick had been losing ground to more commercial breeds. However, the National Trust has been reintroducing it in farms that it controls. Since 1934, the National Trust has owned or controlled virtually the whole of the Buttermere Valley, so there are no intrusive Swaledales or Blackface here. The Lakeland people may be a mix of Briton and Norse, with a bit of Scots thrown in: but the Lakeland sheep is Herdwick.

Ⓐ Immediately across the road from the car park, a signpost 'Ennerdale' indicates the Scarth Gap path. It crosses the valley

Scramblers on Haystacks

START/FINISH:
Gatesgarth NY196150;
farm car park

DISTANCE/ASCENT:
4½ miles (7km) / 2,300ft (700m)

APPROXIMATE TIME:
4½ hours

HIGHEST POINT:
Fleetwith Pike summit 2,100ft (640m)

MAP:
OS Explorer OL4;
OS Landranger 89
Harveys Lakeland West

REFRESHMENTS:
Inns and cafés at Buttermere village (see Walk 18)

ADVICE:
Scrambling on Haystacks is optional. Allow plenty of time for the final descent of Fleetwith as this is rugged and fairly steep. Moreover, the Buttermere view should be lingered over. There is an escape route to Warnscale Bottom alongside the Dubs Beck. Do not attempt to descend towards Buttermere at any other point between Scarth Gap and Fleetwith Pike

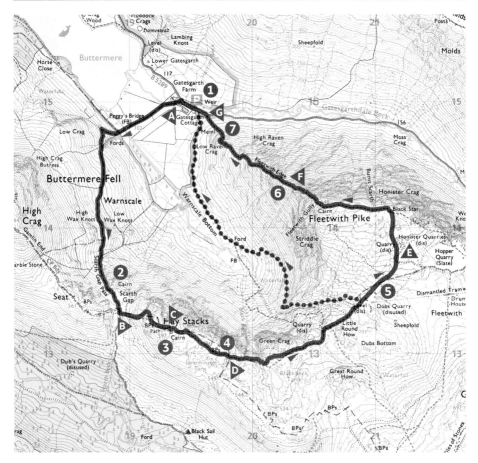

floor, then Peggy's Bridge, and slants uphill to right of a plantation. At the plantation corner, turn sharp left on the main path, to slant up the top edge of the plantation. The path slants all the way up the side of Haystacks, to the large cairn and crossing paths of Scarth Gap.

❷ Scarth Gap NY189133

The pass has formed along fault planes in the underlying rock, and there's hands-on evidence of this on the paths rising to Seat and to Haystacks. On the Haystacks ascent, after the first steep rise and a level section, the pitched path heads up left and then zig-zags back right. On this rightward ascent it crosses a slab where quartz has been scratched and smeared sideways. This effect is called 'slickensides'. The quartz has been melted by the heat of the friction, as one rock mass moves past another.

B At the summit of the Scarth Gap at some rusty iron posts, now the boundary between Allerdale and Copeland, turn sharp left and east.

Looking from Haystacks along Buttermere (with Grasmoor, Walk 20, in the distance)

A pitched path zigzags up the face of Haystacks. More interesting is to leave the path and head straight for the summit. Various small crags offer easy to middling scrambling on good rock.

3 Haystacks Summit NY193132
The summit of Haystacks has two cairns, a tiny tarn, and a view of Pillar, Great Gable, and Buttermere. On Fleetwith Pike, across the hollow of Warnscale Bottom, the junction of Skiddaw Slate (below) and Borrowdale Volcanic (above) can be clearly made out.

C Two or more paths head southeast through knolly ground. They converge to pass the left-hand side of Innominate Tarn.

4 Innominate Tarn NY197129
Many of the early climbers and fell-walkers were Oxford and Cambridge men. They enjoyed such paradoxical names as Nameless Cwm (on the Glyders), the Pic Sans Nom in the Alps, and Innominate – which means 'nameless' in Latin. The name is doubly inappropriate, as Heaton Cooper records the

earlier name of 'Loaf Tarn' – possibly suggested by the three small heather islands.

At the end of the last century, there was a proposal to give it the additional name of 'Wainwright Tarn'. Haystacks was Alfred Wainwright's favourite mountain, and his ashes are scattered near the tarn. Allerdale Council was all for it – the Ordnance Survey said OK – and then they found they'd got the wrong District. The tarn is actually in Copeland.

Guidebook writers do it for fun, for money, and as an excuse to be out on the fells when we should be repainting the bedroom. I certainly don't think we should get our names attached to bits of Lakeland. Hills deserve better than to be called after people. I make an exception for Birkett Fell – see Walk 28.

Innominate Tarn with Great Gable behind

▶ The path passes along the left edge of the tarn, and drops southeast, to contour along a steep slope above Warnscale Bottom and cross the outflow of Blackbeck Tarn. It climbs slightly, to pass to the right of the rock-knolls of Green Crag.

As the path drops towards Dubs Bottom, paths branch off on the left. Ignore these – if you need an escape to Warnscale Bottom, there's a better path just ahead. The main path ahead passes immediately to left of the upstanding knoll of Little Round How (494m spot-height).

Once across Dubs Beck the path turns left and soon starts to drop downstream – this is the best escape route to Buttermere. Otherwise leave the path here to keep ahead, uphill. The spoil heaps of Dubs Quarry are above, with a small hut now used as a mountain refuge. Go straight across a path leading towards the hut, and keep uphill to the left of all the spoil heaps, to find a grassy path uphill.

🟢 Dubs Quarry NY210135

This path was once used by pack ponies, and by quarrymen with their empty sleds on the return journey from Gatesgarthdale. Since the opening of the Honister Tramway in the 1880s it has been forgotten, except as a bridleway line on the map.

The damp mountain ground grows the yellow starry saxifrage and the carnivorous butterwort with its violet flowers. Even the common grassland flowers – milkwort, lousewort, eyebright, tormentil – are a refreshment to the eye after the rocks of Haystacks.

The upper Dubs Quarry has been more recently active, and the pale green colour of the fresh-cut slate can be seen here. There is also a hole in the hill, the exit to one of the quarry shafts.

E The path passes alongside (and to left of) these newer quarry workings. Here you are above the heathery ground, and can head directly uphill (north) to the brink of Honister Crag. A path will be found running to the left, to reach the summit of Fleetwith Pike.

The descent ridge plunges like a loose boulder towards the valley floor 1,600ft (500m) below.

6 Fleetwith Edge NY205143
This is a true glacial arete, its sharp edge formed by lively glaciers in Gatesgarthdale and Warnscale Bottom. The eye follows the line the glacier took, 10,000 years ago, out along the two lakes to the sea. Buzzards and ravens soar in the two valleys. Seeing them from this high ridge makes a nonsense of your bird book, which identifies them only from underneath.

F The path wriggles its way down the sharp ridge, mostly grass and heather but occasionally bare rock. At the very foot of the ridge, at the 225m contour, the direct line is obstructed by Low Raven Crag. Here a cairn stands guard above the sudden steep drop. Turn down sharp right, to the start of a path (partly repaired) which descends in zigzags towards the Honister road.

Descending Fleetwith Edge towards Buttermere

7 Gatesgarth Memorial NY197147
Looking back, you see a white cross just below the crags that block the ridge foot. It commemorates Fanny Mercer, who fell to her death here in 1887. The newspaper account of the accident reveals a particular technique for descending such craggy slopes. Mountaineers then carried, in summer as well as winter, the Alpenstock – a man-high pole with an ice-axe head. The spiked tip of the alpenstock was placed on a lower ledge, and the mountaineer used the shaft for support while jumping down. Miss Mercer, who was only 18, may not have been experienced in the technique: at any rate, she failed to slide her hands down the stick as she jumped, and so was carried forward off the ledge. Without the detailed reporting of the West Cumberland Times, we might not even know that this dubious descent technique had ever been in favour.

G The path joins the road just above Gatesgarth farm.

START/FINISH:
Lanthwaite; car park NY158208

DISTANCE/ASCENT:
6 miles (9.5km) / 3,100ft
(950m)

APPROXIMATE TIME:
6½ hours

HIGHEST POINT:
Grasmoor summit 2,795ft
(852m)

MAP:
OS Explorer OL4;
OS Landranger 89;
Harveys Lakeland West

REFRESHMENTS:
Buttermere village (see Walk
18), or the excellent Kirkstile
Inn at Loweswater (NY141209)

ADVICE:
The initial ascent and final
descent of the route are steep
and stony, to be enjoyed only
by ankles accustomed to
Lakeland terrain. The scramble,
though no harder than such
popular routes as Halls Fell
and Striding Edge, is altogether
more wild. There may be loose
rock in places. While the way
is fairly clear and well-trodden,
if you lose it you may end up
on unpleasant craggy ground.
In winter, it's a serious and
worthwhile mountaineering
expedition

The steep and craggy end of Grasmoor gives a scrambling route that, though easy, has a real mountaineering feel. The return journey is by a sharp and grassy ridge. It may be fairly short, but this is the most serious route in the book.

➊ Crummock Water NY156200

The name is British, 'Crombokwatre', crooked water. The remains of British settlements are still visible around the lake, at Scale Beck and at the foot of Rannerdale.

A From the car park at NY159208, cross the road onto a broad grassy path through the bracken. After 220yds (200m) bear right onto a path through the bracken then bear right onto a path heading southeast up a steepening spur.

At the foot of this path, stop and survey the route ahead. The Grasmoor End Arete is not strictly an arete at all. It is the steep rib that forms the left-hand, northern, edge of the crags of Grasmoor End.

The lower third of the rib is steep scree, with the trodden way visible as a red streak of disturbed stones. The next third is

Grasmoor End

The summit of Crag Hill (Eel Crag), looking towards Skiddaw

rock and heather, rising to a tower. The final third, above the tower, is less steep. Go straight up the scree on small paths to the base of the rocky ground.

❷ Grasmoor End NY165207

This well-drained, steep ground grows luxuriant heather: both bell heather which flowers from late July and the later-flowering ling. The bilberry also flourishes, and as sheep cannot find footing, the purple berries grow big and juicy during July and August. They are good to eat, and an excuse for frequent pauses on the harsh ascent. A similar low twiggy plant but with smaller leaves and red berries is the bearberry (not edible).

The flowers of all this plant-family are dangling bell-shapes. This allows bees to gather nectar as soon as it stops raining, rather than having to wait for the flower to dry out.

B▶ The rocky ground rises in terraces to a triangular buttress. The paths move 22yds (20m) or so to the left along the terraces, then head up into the heather gully to left of this buttress. You can scramble the rocky edge to right of the path.

From the top of the triangular buttress, the rib rises in short rock-steps and heather. The rock-steps can be climbed directly, on well-used holds, or a path zigzags back and forth among them. The rib steepens to the tower already mentioned. The path heads left to bypass this, going up a stony slot. Rocks to right of the path give some more scrambling.

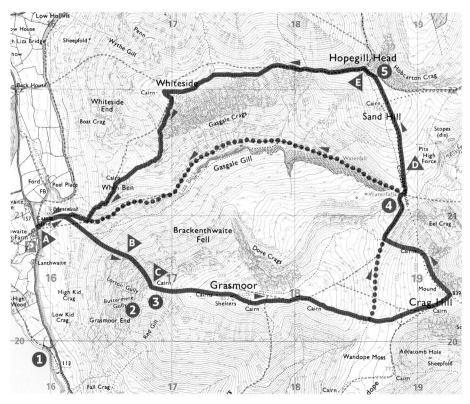

From the top of the tower the rib ascends much more gently, with a sharp rock crest. Where it runs into the main mountain, the path heads left, but easy rocks alongside the drops on the right are a more enjoyable way to reach the grassy plateau above.

❸ Grasmoor End Top NY168204

Craggy places hereabouts provide nest sites for the peregrine falcon – an egg thief fell to his death here. With the elimination of DDT and similar pesticides from the food chain, the peregrine has made a comeback. The casual bird spotter is unlikely to get close enough to distinguish the grey-striped breast, still less the black moustachial streak. Rather, he or she will recognise the various hunting birds by their jizz, which refers to their general characteristics, shape and size. The peregrine, with its stubby wings and rapid wing beats, has something of the style of a pigeon or grouse. When disturbed, it flies with a series of rapid angry squawks, flapping briskly straight out from the hillside towards the opposite side of the valley.

Hopegill Head, seen here from
the north; the route drops along
the right skyline

In the same way, the hawk that somewhat resembles a
seagull is the hen harrier. The buzzard is the one that soars.
The first few eagles that you see are, in fact, buzzards.
Once you know your buzzard, an eagle will be instantly
recognisable, as its slow wing beats reveal it to be a much
bigger and more distant bird.

Gentle slopes, and occasional cairns, lead east to
Grasmoor summit. This has a shelter cairn with nooks in
three directions. The path continues east into the wide col of
Wandope Moss, then climbs to Crag Hill (perversely renamed
as Eel Crag by Wainwright).

Crag Hill's stone trig point is just starting to disintegrate.
The plateau runs away northwest, becoming a ridgeline
descending north. Just above Coledale Hause, the path drops
off to the left in scree zigzags, descending through some
rather awkward broken ground. (In mist or wet, an easier
descent from Crag Hill is to head back the path you came on,
down to the col of Wandope Moss, and turn right down the
wide crossing path.)

In the little valley between Crag Hill and Grasmoor, a wider
path runs down to right of a stream. Follow this downhill, but
where the main path and the stream turn down left, keep
ahead to the col of Coledale Hause.

④ Coledale Hause NY189212
This can be an impressive place on a stormy day, with cloud
rising out of Gasgale Gill, whisking through the pass and
dropping into Coledale. In such weather a left turn here, to
follow the stream down Gasgale Gill, is an escape route.

On the ridge of Whiteside at the end of the walk, looking up at the Grasmoor End Arete. Crummock Water behind.

D▶ A fairly clear path climbs northwards out of the pass to the flat summit of Sand Hill. A shallow dip and slight climb lead to the rocky top of Hopegill Head.

⑤ Hopegill Head NY186222

This is a fine top perched above northern drops. Skiddaw Slate forms slippery flat stones: the summit cairn can rise no more than 20in (50cm) before starting to slide away over the edge. Also typical of the Skiddaw Slate is the sharp ridge leading to Whiteside, and the way that its occasional rocky bits are smooth and slippery. Skiddaw Slate scree lies on the ledges of the final descent to Whin Ben.

E▶ From Hopegill Head a path leads along the westward ridge. Most of the occasional rocky moments can be avoided by a path on the right, though when dry they present no difficulty. The slatey rock is slightly treacherous when wet.

The ridge becomes grassier as it climbs to the 719m point labelled as 'Whiteside' on the Harveys map. This point has no cairn, and Wainwright and the Ordnance Survey consider Whiteside to be the 707m spot height reached after another ¼ mile (400m). From here the descent is unclear at first. The direction is southwest, with scree on the right and steep drops on the left. A path soon forms as the descent spur steepens. The ridge turns slightly right, and becomes rocky, with scree lying on the ledges. It levels, then rises briefly to Whin Ben.

From Whin Ben the path drops steeply again down a spur to Liza Beck, where there's a footbridge not seen from above (NY163210). The grass path ahead runs to the car park.

Skiddaw

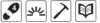

Skiddaw is a tall pile of little flat stones. The direct route from Keswick, though popular, is not exciting. A start-point round the back, at Bassenthwaite, gives a ridge walk on the way up and a waterfall on the way down.

❶ Field Studies NY231323
Unusually for the National Park, this walk starts on field paths that are so little used as to be invisible on the ground. Such walking requires careful work with map and compass to find the next stile at each field end. The field paths below the flowering hedgerows make a pleasant setting to start and end this walk in the high stony places.

To avoid stile-hunting fun, use the alternative start from the minor road above High Side (NY236310) where there is a roadside pull-off at the foot of the bridleway path.

A▶ From the corner of the village green, follow the road south and fork left onto a very minor road called Burthwaite. Where this bends left after 220yds (200m), there are two stone stiles on the right. Take the second of these. Straight away the path crosses Chapel Beck at a footbridge, then turns left, upstream. After 55yds (50m) it slants up right, through a strip of woodland to a stile at its top edge.

Looking across the rooftops of Keswick to Skiddaw

START/FINISH:
Bassenthwaite (NY230322); car parking around village green. Those who want to eliminate the initial field paths can park at Peter House Farm (NY249323) or near High Side (NY236310). To avoid the road walk from Peter House, pick up the bridleway (NY245319), which cuts through Hole House and Barkbeth to High Side

DISTANCE/ASCENT:
10 miles (16km) / 3,000ft (900m)

APPROXIMATE TIME:
7 hours

HIGHEST POINT:
Skiddaw summit 3,054ft (931m)

MAP:
OS Explorer OL4;
OS Landranger 89 or 90;
Harveys Lakeland North

REFRESHMENTS:
Sun Inn, Bassenthwaite

ADVICE:
In winter, the scree-struggle holds its snow, and it crosses a high and steep slope. An ice axe may be required. At any time, Skiddaw's high and separated summit is even more exposed to wind and weather than all the others and the steep terrain includes loose shale

❷ Bassenthwaite Lake NY224287

Bassenthwaite Lake starts to appear beyond the nearer hedges, and this gives something interesting to look at apart from the grey screes of Skiddaw overhead. Bassenthwaite is famous as Lakeland's only lake – the others all being either Waters (like Derwentwater) or Meres (like Thirlmere). Actually, Windermere is now often called 'Lake Windermere', but this is strictly incorrect as 'mere' already means 'lake'.

Heading up Longside Edge in
dodgy-looking winter weather

While working on 'Morte d' Arthur', Tennyson stayed with his
friend James Spedding of Mirehouse. It may be that the lake
of the poem, with its 'zigzag paths and juts of pointed rock',
reflects the scenery of Bassenthwaite. Lakeland is one of the
few parts of Britain without its own Arthur legend – possibly
because the country is romantic enough without the help
of Merlin, Galahad and the gang. The closest Arthur myth,
a particularly implausible one, has the Round Table in an
alfresco setting near Penrith.

B▸ The way follows fences up southeast. After a stile, turn
right along the fence to another stile, then a gate with a
waymark pointing left. Head up beside the fence without
going through the gate. A track joins from the right. After
55yds (50m), look out for a stile and footbridge down right,
and slant up across a field to the hill road.

Turn right onto the road for ¹/₃ mile (600m) to a lay-by and
finger post pointing back left. The wide green path slants up
a field. After 220yds (200m), and before the end of the field,
waymark arrows mark a path junction. Turn directly uphill,
beside the remains of a hedge, bearing left after 220yds
(200m) to a field gate. Continue around the hillside to a ladder
stile and a clear green track running into the Southerndale
valley. After a gate and stile, turn right, off the track, onto
the ridge crest above, to reach the high point of Ullock Pike.

❸ Ullock Pike NY244287
The Skiddaw Slate that forms the northern part of the Lake
District was originally a muddy sediment in the ocean trench

Derwent Water from Carl Side

separating Scotland and England. (The rocks of the Central Fells, known as the Borrowdale Volcanic, were a chain of volcanic islands off the English shore.) Skiddaw Slate is brittle. It forms no great rock faces, but long slopes of scree. From Ullock Pike you can look across Bassenthwaite Lake to the Grasmoor Group and appreciate the particular shape of the Skiddaw Slate sort of hill. Uncluttered by the crags and rocky lumps of the central fells, high smooth slopes rise steeply to elegant ridges. In the other direction, looking up at Skiddaw, we can see the typical Skiddaw Slate scree. We shall encounter that scree more intimately in an hour or so. Meanwhile, Ullock Pike has rocky hollows for eating sandwiches in.

C The ridge turns east and broadens to the flat top of Carl Side. A path curves round to the left, alongside the drops into Southerndale, to Carlside Tarn (often dry) then slants up to the left. After half an hour of hard work, it reaches the ridge top at a sprawling shelter-cairn. Skiddaw's final trig is 110yds (100m) north, beyond a small col.

④ Skiddaw Summit NY260291

As well as the trig point there is a viewpoint table, and Skiddaw, standing almost alone at the northern edge of Lakeland, is a superb viewpoint. Long ridges of the Southern Uplands of Scotland and the Pennines are seen, and on a clear day the Isle of Man and even Ireland. According to the poet Macaulay, 'the red fires on Skiddaw roused the burghers of Carlisle' to warn them of the Spanish Armada; and here was one of a chain of just 12 fires that were lit from the south coast to the north of Scotland to celebrate the Queen's Silver Jubilee in 1978.

Skiddaw was one of the earliest Lakeland mountains to be ascended for pleasure. Then, as now, the main way of ascent was by the 'Pony Path' straight up out of Keswick, and at the summit you are likely to be joined by many walkers who have come up that way. It is an arduous and relatively unrewarding route, especially during the last 100 years or so since the refreshment hut disappeared from the slope of Jenkin Hill.

D From the summit continue north, down slopes that are stony but not particularly steep, then flatten to a small plateau. A small path descends slightly east of north, with a fence on the right, on grassy slopes. A slight rise and cairn indicate the summit of Bakestall.

5 Bakestall NY266307

We have entered the quiet country known as 'Back o' Skiddaw', where paths are small and folk are few. 'Caldbeck Hills are worth all England else', Wainwright quotes approvingly but he was writing the introduction to his 'Northern Fells' at the time, and had some interest in promoting sales. Back o' Skiddaw is grassy, and peaty, and heathery. The hills are smooth and soothing, the place to come if you need to calm down after the excitements of the Borrowdale Volcanic.

Peak-baggers in Lakeland generally bag Wainwrights, and will be glad to know that Bakestall, as well as Ullock Pike, Long Side and Carl Side, are all tops that can be ticked off the list.

E▶ Retrace your steps from the cairn for 55yds (50m) to rejoin the fence, which now descends northeast. Go down beside the fence; or 55yds (50m) left of it, for the sake of the view over the top of a loose and unexpected crag, and along the valley of Dash Beck. At the slope's foot join a stony track beside the Dash Beck.

Whitewater Dash foot

6 Whitewater Dash NY272314

The Whitewater Dash waterfall is just below this track. It can be peered into, adventurously, from various perches. Indeed, if you happen to be accompanied by a mortal enemy, this is the ideal spot for that final life-or-death struggle. Or you can wander down the track and enjoy the waterfall from a distance, while finishing the sandwiches.

F▶ The downhill track leads out along the deep-scooped valley to the tarred track of Dash Farm. Here, quite suddenly, it leaves the Lake District. The mountains are left behind, and green fields are all around. A crag opposite has a wide vein of white quartz. Turn left along the tarred track, or on the short grass alongside, to reach the public road and a small carpark after ²/₃ mile (1km). If you started at the High Side car park, rather than at Bassenthwaite village, turn left here along the road.

7 Bridleway Peter House Farm NY249324

Because it is a bridleway, and not a footpath, each of its stiles has a gate alongside. This is a useful general hint for identifying field paths: if there's a stile but no gate, you're on a footpath not a bridleway. Remorseful knees, equally, may appreciate this subtlety.

According to British Rail regulations, a typewriter was a musical instrument and a tortoise was an insect. Even today,

Skiddaw and Long Side from walk start at Bassenthwaite village

a cello counts as a child, as does a pair of skis. In the same way, a bicycle is taken to be a horse for pathway purposes. If you meet a mountain bike on a path that isn't a bridleway you're entitled to scowl and mutter rude words.

G The bridleway continues directly opposite: it is signed 'Bassenthwaite 2 miles', purely to discourage those who don't look at maps – the distance is actually 2km, just over a mile. Follow the farm track for 33yds (30m) only, then bear left, past a waymark post.

This bridleway is little-used, but is marked with white-topped poles at stiles. It crosses open field and passes a single plane tree to a stile. Keep ahead at a four-way signpost, and cross three stiles with a fence on the left. At a line of five oaks, white paint-spots indicate that you should head out for 55yds (50m) into the field, then turn down the middle of two fields towards the village. This differs from the path indicated on the OS map. Go through an unmarked gate, and down with fence on your right. Now a gate leads onto a track that drops to the village green.

Blencathra

In all Lakeland, Blencathra is the place to take someone who isn't sure if they're going to like hill walking. And the place on Blencathra to take them is Halls Fell Ridge. The first 1,000ft (300m) of ascent may be steep and stony, but after that Halls Fell becomes a sharp scrambly edge that simply climbs itself.

❶ Threlkeld NY320253
The reason for Threlkeld is the granite quarry, visible across the valley on the lower slopes of Clough Head. Now it serves walkers on a single hill – Blencathra – and is one of the quieter Lakeland villages.

The wide slope of Blencathra above has acted as a spectral screen for ghostly projections. On three separate Midsummer's Eves, troops of riders, accompanied by horsedrawn coaches, have flitted across the hill. The most recent sighting was in 1745, the year of Prince Charlie's invasion. Perhaps the existence of the Scottish Parliament may induce another appearance.

A▶ The route starts from the car park within the village. (The one on Blease Road above the village is an alternative – from it head uphill, then turn right along the fell foot path.) Head east through the village, passing both pubs. At the village end, bear left up a steep little lane. After ¼ mile (400m), a bridleway path leads up to the left. It heads uphill, with

Blencathra from Great Mell Fell

START/FINISH:
Car park (with toilets) in Threlkeld village NY319253

DISTANCE/ASCENT:
6 miles (9.5km) / 2,500ft (750m)

APPROXIMATE TIME:
5½ hours

HIGHEST POINT:
Blencathra summit 2,848ft (868m)

MAP:
OS Explorer OL5;
OS Landranger 90;
Harveys Lakeland North

REFRESHMENTS:
Inns at Threlkeld, Scales (White Horse); cafés at Keswick

ADVICE:
The scrambling on Halls Fell is easy, but above high, steep slopes. It is possible to get into difficulties by attempting to pass round below the rocksteps rather than climbing over them. The route is suitable for a sensible 8-year old – I have taken my own up it – but not for the more sedentary sort of dog. It becomes serious under icy conditions. Sharp Edge (an optional diversion) is for confident scramblers only

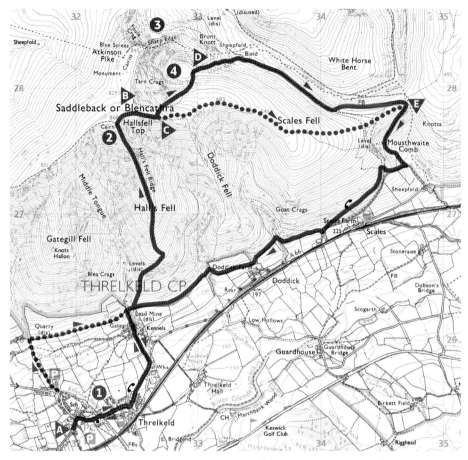

a stream down to its right, and passes Gategill farm to reach open fell at the foot of Gate Gill's little valley slot.

The steep heather slope to right of the little valley is the foot of Halls Fell. Head up the steep, stony path. Half an hour of tough, tiring work brings you to the foot of the rocky ridge.

Bravely straight up the front is the easy way to go here – but note that this principle does not necessarily apply to real life away from Blencathra. The ridge hauls you rapidly upwards and deposits you like a lift set for 'roof' at the very summit.

❷ Blencathra Summit NY324277

The summit boasts a feeble cairn: the flat, slippery Skiddaw Slate isn't good for dry-stone structures. There is also the concrete ring of a former surveying station.

The last hill in Lakeland to remain unnamed was High Raise, above Langdale. Until about 1950 this was referred to only as High White Stones, which is actually a nearby sheepfold. But for far longer than that, Blencathra has had two separate names. At the dawn of written history, which in Lakeland hill terms is the mid-eighteenth century, the mountain was known as 'Saddleback'. This is the shape of it as seen from the A66 coming in from Penrith. It was Wordsworth who discovered and promoted the earlier name 'Blencathra' – which means 'Hill of the Chair', and the Celt who bestowed it was again probably approaching along the A66. Wainwright continued the campaign, so that nearly everyone now says 'Blencathra'. Those who think a correct and authentic name is more important than what places are actually called should note that 200 years ago, the tarn on Blencathra was 'Purple Tarn'. Call it by its proper name, and have fun being misunderstood by every walker in England.

Scramblers on Halls Fell silhouetted against St John's Vale and distant Thirlmere

B▶ A path leads eastwards from the summit, with the steep drop of the mountain's splendid south face on the right. After 220yds (200m), a path to the left would take you to Sharp Edge descent. Continue on eastwards, however, until Scales Tarn comes into sight below on the left, with a steep zigzag path leading down to it.

③ Sharp Edge NY327284

There are no rock climbs on the Skiddaw Slate: but the ridge now visible on the opposite side of Scales Tarn is the nearest thing, being a classic scramble line. There's a geological reason for this better stone. A huge bubble of molten rock rose through the slates a few miles to the north of here. As it solidified to form a great lump of underground granite, the heat cooked the surrounding rocks and made them tougher. (The geological term for this ring of hardened rock around an intrusion is 'metamorphic aureole'.)

The tip of the underground granite is exposed at one or two places in the valley of the Caldew. Its full hugeness is disclosed by measuring the force of gravity: the granite is slightly less heavy than its surroundings. The reduction in the Earth's pull reduces the weight of the average hill walker by about 3g. This makes no appreciable difference to the difficulty of ascending Blencathra.

C▶ The tarn is pretty, but the descent to it is quite steep: you could avoid it by continuing east down the gentle ridge, with big drops on your left, right down to the Mousthwaite col (**E▶**).

The more interesting but slightly more demanding route takes in Scales Tarn and the Glenderaterra valley side. Descend the loose, zigzag path on the left to Scales Tarn's outflow.

④ Scales Tarn NY329281

In past centuries it was thought that Blencathra was a volcano, with Scales Tarn, which was bottomless and reflected the stars at midday, being the former crater. Today we know that Blencathra's rocks actually formed at the bottom of a deep trench under a previous version of the Atlantic Ocean. And Scales Tarn, with its steep headwall, its bounding ridges, its easterly view and its deep-hole-half-way-to-the-sky feel, is a typical glaciated corrie with ice-plucked floor. Disappointingly, the bottomless tarn is nowhere more than 33ft (10m) deep.

While most will be content to dabble their toes in the tarn, a few may be inspired to return to the summit by way of Sharp Edge. This is not difficult as scrambles go (unless conditions are windy or icy), but it is very exposed and falling off it can be fatal. A path climbs from the foot of the tarn, and continues just below the crest on the right, though it is better to follow the good rocks of the crest itself. Where the ridge butts against the main mountain a shallow groove leads upwards. Do not bear left onto treacherous gravelly ground but go straight on up clean, well-used rock to the top.

On Halls Fell Ridge on a winter afternoon

Scales Tarn

D From Scales Tarn's outflow, follow the small splashy stream down out of the hollow. The path goes down beside – or if you prefer, inside – the stream, then turns right to wander horizontally along the side of the Glenderamackin valley, which is almost as long as its name. The path stays high above the valley stream, to reach the col at the head of Mousthwaite Comb (NY347279).

E Here there is a choice of descending paths. The one going down inside the combe is nicer than the one out on its right. The path drops towards a small car park ²/₃ mile (1km) east of the White Horse Inn at Scales. Tired members of the party can wait in the car park or the inn while energetic members fetch the car.

Those energetic members will turn off just above the road, up a bracken slope on the right. A small path runs westwards, immediately above the tops of the enclosed fields. The path leads back around the bottom of Blencathra, looking down on a farmhouse and the A66, up at Halls Fell Ridge, spiky against the sky, and forward to the sunset and Cat Bells.

It rejoins the outward route at the foot of Halls Fell ridge.

The Dodds

The Dodds, north of Helvellyn, form a wide grassy ridge with great views. Anywhere else in England, that would be enough. In the Lakes, though, we can afford to be more demanding. As well as the grassy ridge we can ask for an exciting approach through craggy ground, and a return along a miners' path perched high above Ullswater.

START/FINISH:
Dockray (NY393216) – small car park at the southern end of the village opposite a telephone box

DISTANCE/ASCENT:
Main route: 13 miles (21km) / 3,000ft (900m);
Shorter version: 9½ miles (15.5km) / 2,300ft (700m)

APPROXIMATE TIME:
Main route: 8½ hours
Short version: 5 hours

HIGHEST POINT:
Great Dodd Summit 2,815ft (858m)

MAP:
OS Explorer OL5;
OS Landranger 90
Harveys Lakeland Central

REFRESHMENTS:
Royal Hotel, Dockray

ADVICE:
The second, low-level part of the walk is trickier than the first. Be sure to have enough daylight for the Glencoyndale miners' path, which is narrow and crosses a high, steep slope. The longer version has a more interesting ascent route and is preferable. However, its ascent onto Clough Head is difficult in icy conditions

1 Dockray NY393216

Dockray is a tiny village tucked into a fold of the eastern fells, out of sight of busy Ullswater. It is merely a few farms and an inn. That inn (a particularly good one) hints at its former importance as the first point of civilisation after the high and wild crossing of the Old Coach Road from Keswick. Old coaching prints decorate its walls.

The busy life of today has barely touched Dockray. Last time I came down the lane, I spent 20 minutes with a uniformed police officer driving stray lambs back into their field.

The beck through Dockray descends to Ullswater by way of the Aira Force. A path from Dockray goes down to left of the stream, and is a good way to admire this fine waterfall with its two rustic stone bridges. When the stream is full, spray from the fall envelopes the lower bridge – but in such weather you were wearing your waterproofs anyway. There is a car park, with small café, where the stream arrives at Ullswater.

The Dodds ridge continues over White Side towards Helvellyn

Great Dodd at dawn

A A signpost 'Dowthwaitehead' indicates a steep lane rising out of Dockray. After 1 mile (1.6km) the road reaches a T-junction: a gate ahead leads onto a rough, rutted track.

② Old Coach Road NY345231

Horse-drawn traffic used this high line to avoid soft ground in the Vale of Threlkeld. The fine views across to Blencathra and Skiddaw, and along the Vale of Keswick, were quite irrelevant. It has found new favour as a long-distance route, being a 'very rough off road alternative' on the cyclists' Coast-to-Coast developed by Sustrans. Bikers who use it to finish a long first day from Whitehaven will arrive at the Royal Hotel with exactly the same feelings of relief as early coach travellers.

B longer version The longer walk follows the Old Coach Road for 3½ miles (5.5km) as it climbs around the flank of Matterdale Common and Clough Head. It reaches its highest point on the northeast ridge of Clough Head, descends and then levels before its final descent to St Johns in the Vale. Descend to a gate in a fence across the track, pass through the gate and turn left up the re-entrant (a tiny valley), passing through Clough Fold (sheepfold) NY332235. At the top of this final slope, a green re-entrant runs up left to a rocky col between Threlkeld Knotts and the main mountain. From this col a narrow path slants up right, among small outcrops, to reach gentle grass slopes to the west of Clough Head.

From Clough Head's stone trig a wide grass path leads south into a wide col. It passes to the left of the rocky knoll of Calfhow Pike then climbs to Great Dodd, point **③**.

Sunrise over the Dodds

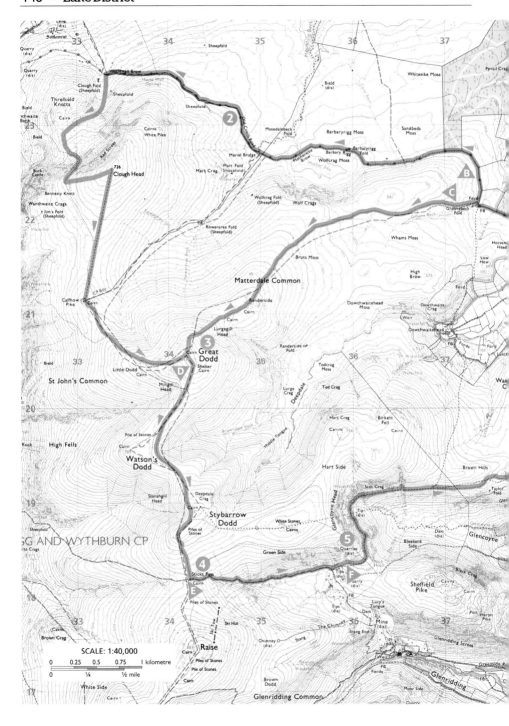

▷ **shorter version** This follows the Old Coach Road for just 660yds (600m) to the ford and footbridge of Groove Beck. A faint grassy path climbs to right of the stream, then moves gradually away from it to the ridge crest. It follows the ridge up to a small cairn, and the shelter cairn of Great Dodd just beyond.

③ Great Dodd NY342205

The wide grass ridge over the Dodds is the easiest high-level walking in Lakeland, and popular in winter with skiers. Lakeland's only ski lift is on the slope of Raise. The ridge runs on over Helvellyn, and dips below the 2,000ft (600m) mark briefly at Grisedale Tarn before continuing over Fairfield as far as Red Screes for a sudden descent to Ambleside.

▷ Leave Great Dodd southwards, to find the path after a few metres. A right fork leads out to Watson's Dodd, but the left-hand path, along the brink of Deepdale, is more interesting. The paths are clear on a clear day, but tricky in mist. After Stybarrow Dodd the path drops to a col where a cairned path crosses the ridge.

④ Sticks Pass NY342182

The Helvellyn Ridge presents a formidable obstacle to anyone seeking to pass from Ullswater to Keswick. At 2,450ft (750m) Sticks Pass was the highest pass used by ordinary people, hill walkers apart. Pack ponies came this way from the Greenside Mines, loaded with ore for the smelting works of Derwentwater. The name indicates that the pass was waymarked with wooden posts.

This was the site of an annual 'Meet', an enjoyable get-together where shepherds from St John's Vale and Matterdale returned each other's strayed sheep.

▶ Turn left at the pass, and take the rather rough path that runs gently down into the valley of the Sticks Gill (east). The path keeps to the left side as far as the foot of the upper valley, to reach a clump of five cairns below the two huge holes marked on some OS maps as 'disused quarry'.

⑤ Gilgowars Level NY359185

Disused quarry it isn't. Among the spoil heaps just below it is the entrance to the Gilgowers mine level. This collapsed spectacularly in 1862 – fortunately on a Sunday, so the workings were empty. The holes in the hill are still slowly growing as the underground workings fill with rubble.

The floor of the valley is covered in spoil from the Gilgowers Level, and from High Horse Level just downhill. The first of the Greenside lead mines were opened here in the seventeenth century, and worked by hand and by pony. There were cottages along the beck, inhabited from spring to autumn.

The stream was dammed to provide water for the water wheels of the crushing plant. This dam burst in the 1870s.

Sheffield Pike from
Ullswater Steamer

Ullswater dawn, seen from
Sheffield Pike

A 66lb (30kg) lump of silver from the refining works was
washed away, and there is no record of its ever having been
recovered.

▶ Turn left and leave the path at the cairns at the foot of this
upper valley, and make your way up to a point just below the
huge 'disused quarry' hole. Here a small path contours out
to the right. It passes 100ft (40m) vertically above the col
of Nick Head, with the outlying hill of Sheffield Pike beyond
the col. (The diversion to Sheffield Pike is worthwhile for the
view all the way along Ullswater to Cross Fell in the Pennines,
and also for sheltered picnic sites between the rocks.)

The small path contours round the head of Glencoyne. The
valley head is steep and rocky, and many streams splash across
the path. It continues on the same level along the northern
wall of the valley, where the slope eventually becomes less
steep. The path crosses a wall (rebuilt by the NT Estate
Team) and eases up to the left, crossing grassy moorland for
1/3 mile (500m) and dropping to meet another wall.

The path runs to the left, above the wall, for 1 mile (1.6km).
Below the wall the slope steepens as it drops to Ullswater.
On the slope of Common Fell the wall turns slightly right and
starts to descend: here continue straight ahead for 220yds
(200m). The ground drops ahead, with a view down to
Dockray. Go straight down the slope, joining a small stream
(the Pounder Sike). A path alongside the stream leads to a
gate into the village.

Helvellyn Edges

Helvellyn is England's most popular mountain, and Striding Edge probably the most popular route up it. And rightly so: it's a splendid rocky ridge, with big drops on either side and easy scrambling along the top.

START/FINISH:
Large pay-and-display car park in Glenridding (NY385169)

DISTANCE/ASCENT:
8 miles (12.5km) / 3,000ft (900m)

APPROXIMATE TIME:
7 hours

HIGHEST POINT:
Helvellyn summit 950m (3,116ft)

MAP:
OS Explorer OL5;
OS Landranger 90;
Harveys Lakeland Central

REFRESHMENTS:
Cafés and inns in Glenridding

ADVICE:
Striding Edge under snow is a serious proposition, as the path below the crest is lost and the crest itself is trampled hard, even icy. Crampons and ice axes are often advisable. It is also dangerous in strong winds. Ordinary rainfall need not deter an ascent, as the rock is firm and clean, giving good grip even when wet. The same cautions apply to Swirral Edge

On this route we save Striding Edge for the descent. The scrambling is slightly easier in that direction, the views are even better, and towards the end of the day it becomes a little less crowded.

① Glenridding NY386169

Glenridding is a busy little village. Indeed, on a sunny summer Saturday, you could call it crawling. PT Barnum reduced crowding at his wild animal show with a large sign 'to the Egress': those who went to see what it was found themselves out on the street. Similarly, every signpost in Glenridding seems to indicate 'Helvellyn'.

It's odd to find so Scottish a name as Glenridding among the Norse. It may actually derive from the Celtic, a language related to Scots Gaelic – or it may reflect a patch of ground taken over permanently by Scots raiders who decided to stay.

A ▶ Turn right out of the car park to cross Glenridding Beck on the main road. A rough track on the right runs beside the stream. After 330yds (300m), when the track forks, keep right by the stream (signposted Greenside) for another ⅓ mile (500m) to Rattlebeck Bridge.

Helvellyn: Striding Edge ahead, Swirral Edge on the right

❷ Rattlebeck Bridge NY379168

This bridge was swept away in October 1927, when the dam at Keppelcove Tarn burst, 2 miles (3km) upstream and nearly 2,000ft (500m) above. A wall of water 7ft (2m) high hit Glenridding: furniture was carried right across Ullswater, but most of the inhabitants were in bed on upper floors and no lives were lost.

Even the normal flow down Glenridding Beck imparted a greenish tinge to Ullswater as long as the mines were still at work. Mine gravel extended the alluvial fan of the beck into the lake by 10ft (3m) a year.

▶ Do not cross Rattlebeck Bridge, but take a little tarred lane uphill to a gate. A small footpath leads off to the right (signposted Greenside road). It crosses fields with waymarks and narrow gates, to join the track up Glen Ridding (the valley). Turn left, to pass the youth hostel and camping barn, and pass below the spoil heaps of the lower Greenside mines. At the junction of the tracks, keep to the left (signposted Red Tarn and Helvellyn).

❸ Greenside Mines NY365175

Walk 23 (the Dodds) passes the older workings in the Sticks Valley, 1,000ft (300m) above. During the 1830s Lucy Tongue Level was opened up, and crushing and smelting operations were set up at this lower site. The youth hostel was originally built for miners.

During the nineteenth century tarns all along the face of Helvellyn were dammed to provide water and hydroelectric power for mine machinery: Red Tarn was raised by 3ft (1m),

Swirral Edge

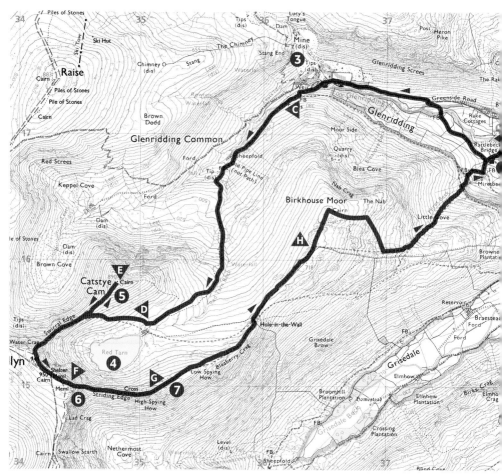

Striding Edge: a serious place in winter

and tarns were created in Brown Cove and Keppel Cove. In 1890 the mines had electric winding gear and the world's first electric locomotive. Thousands worked here, producing 3,000 tons of lead ore a year and about a ton of silver. The last mine closed in 1962.

Given the two dam bursts and the spectacular collapse of Gilgower, we may feel that Greenside would have benefited from interference by the Health & Safety Executive. In the seventeenth and eighteenth centuries early death, whether at work or at home, was a part of everyday life. Our levels of industrial safety are a modern luxury, and would have stopped the Industrial Revolution in its iron tracks. (Incidentally, if hill walking were an industrial activity the HSE would certainly put a stop to it.)

 A footbridge on the left crosses the Keppelcove Beck, with a well-built path continuing upstream. Steep cones of Birkhouse Moor and Catstye Cam tower over the path. It crosses Redtarn Beck, and runs up to the tarn itself.

❹ Red Tarn NY350154

Coleridge called Helvellyn 'this prodigious wildness', and a print made in his day shows eagles over Red Tarn. It's hard to imagine that the body of Charles Gough, who fell from Striding Edge in 1805, could have lain undiscovered for three months. Tourists started coming to Red Tarn to visit the melancholy scene of his fall. Since then, on only the wettest of days has there not been a human presence at Red Tarn. Now, the wet day would also have to be midweek and in winter.

The tarn's head wall rising 1,000ft (300m) to the summit of Helvellyn, the two bounding aretes and the pointed peak of Catstye Cam, make this a perfect glaciated corrie for geography students and an impressive spot for the rest of us as well.

▶ From the foot of Red Tarn the path heads up to the right, to reach the low point of the ridge between Helvellyn and Catstye Cam. Swirral Edge is ahead, but first a diversion can be made to Catstye Cam. A small path runs along the ridge, which is narrow but not rocky.

❺ Catstye Cam NY347157

Catstye Cam (Catstycam) is a fine narrow summit, poised above Glenridding and Keppel Cove. A sandwich break here will allow the densest crowds to finish coming up Striding Edge. The old name is Catechedam. The meaning is as obscure as the spelling.

▶ Return down the southwest ridge, and go up Swirral Edge. This is rocky but not difficult, with a choice of routes among projections of splintery stone. It arrives right beside the summit of Helvellyn. Just down to the left is the cross-shaped shelter where most people stop for lunch.

Striding Edge, Summer,
St Sunday Crag behind

Continue along the plateau edge for 160yds (150m), to the triangular monument above Striding Edge.

⑥ Gough Monument NY344150

Striding Edge is a classic example of an arete: the sharp edge and very steep sides were formed by two small corrie-glaciers eating away on either side. The crest is good rock, with plenty of holds, but it is narrow in places, and the drops are considerable.

The triangular cairn is a memorial to the first recorded person to fall off it, one Gough, in April of 1805. There was new snow on the rocks at the time. The sad story of his faithful dog standing guard over his decaying corpse was set in verse by Sir Walter Scott and also by Wordsworth and has been repeated in every subsequent guidebook, including this one!

▶ Go straight down over the edge below the monument cairn, on various eroded and scree-covered paths. Soon this unpleasant ground becomes the sound rock of the ridge itself. A path on the left-hand (Red Tarn) side avoids the difficulties. For those taking the crest direct, the crux is the second short ascent. This is taken on large well-worn holds in a shallow groove round on the right.

⑦ Striding Edge NY349149

Another memorial, set beside a comfortable lunch-nook in the ridge crest, marks where the second person fell over the edge. (One Dixon, following the Patterdale foxhounds in 1858.) At this point the commemoration of accident victims was brought to an end – fortunately, as otherwise the ridge would now be seriously obstructed. On a sunny summer Sunday 500 people ascend Striding Edge, and every few years someone dies in the attempt.

G▶ Soon after the second memorial the Edge turns back into an ordinary ridge. A broad path, slightly down on the Red Tarn side, leads northeast for ²/₃ mile (1km) to the corner of a wall. A path to Glenridding goes down through the wall gap, but a nicer path keeps ahead, to left of the wall, towards Birkhouse Moor.

H▶ The wall bends right, downhill, and older maps show the right of way as following it down. However, a new path now keeps straight ahead to the summit of Birkhouse Moor, before descending eastwards in well-built zigzags. It joins Mires Beck and goes down beside it towards Glenridding, rejoining the outward route just above the village.

Helvellyn edges from Fairfield

START/FINISH:
Main car park at Ambleside
(NY376047)

DISTANCE/ASCENT:
11 miles (18km) / 3,100ft
(950m)

APPROXIMATE TIME:
7½ hours

HIGHEST POINT:
Fairfield summit 2,864ft (873m)

MAP:
OS Explorer OL5 and OL7;
OS Landranger 90;
Harveys Lakeland Central

REFRESHMENTS:
Many cafés, restaurants and
inns at Ambleside

ADVICE:
Those who like to get as high
as possible as soon as possible
could omit the Scandale Valley
by following the path from
High Sweden Bridge to Low
Pike, then follow the ridge to
Dove Crag

Fairfield, which fittingly means 'pleasant fell', is often walked by one of its horseshoe routes either on the ridges surrounding Rydal Beck or on those surrounding Deepdale. This is a variation of the former, choosing to follow an ancient traders' route up Scandale to its pass before taking to delightful mountain ridges.

❶ Ambleside NY374046
Ambleside's oldest buildings are clustered around the Kirkstone Road, where cobbled alleys run off the narrow lane, hemmed in by the hillslopes of Wansfell and Red Screes. Streams that gush down the steep fellsides once powered water wheels for local corn mills. There is a restored wheel by Stock Beck near the North Road. Nearby is Bridge House, a tiny sixteenth-century dwelling built over Stock Beck. It was once used as a storehouse for apples, and was part of the Ambleside Hall estate. The hall, sadly, is long gone. Since then the little house has been a tearoom, a cobbler's and a gift shop, but is now a National Trust information centre.

The poet William Wordsworth once had an office, the Old Stamp House, next to the bakery on the corner of Church Street and Lake Road.

A▸ From the car park, cross the Grasmere road and go up Smithy Brow. Take Sweden Bridge Road, the second lane on the left, and follow it northwards past pretty Lakeland cottages of stone and slates. The road ends at a gate, where a stony track continues north into the valley of Scandale Beck.

❷ High Sweden Bridge NY379067
Though it's hidden by trees, you can hear Scandale Beck as it rushes over its rocky bed far below. There's a short detour to the left to see High Sweden Bridge, a one-arched packhorse bridge, where the beck tumbles over boulders beneath woods of birch, holly, ash and alder. If you're lucky you'll hear longtailed and marsh tits chattering in the trees. Beyond the far banks, bracken-cloaked hillslopes rise to the crags of Low Pike, the end of a ridge thrown out by Dove Crag.

B▸ Although a tempting path across the bridge makes for the Low Pike ridge, our route continues up Scandale, and so you

High Sweden Bridge

will need to retrace your steps back to the main track. Head northwards along it through a landscape that quickly loses its prettiness to be replaced by stark desolation.

❸ Upper Scandale NY378083
The woodland has gone, replaced by bare, craggy slopes with thin moor grasses. A cairn, the High Beckstones (Bakestones on OS maps), juts out from the rocky flanks of Scandale Head. The path is wetter, now bound by dark, ragged dry-stone walls, while the beck meanders lazily through rushes and reeds. Ravens may be scouring the hillsides or quarrelling with some buzzard.

C▶ At Scandale Bottom the track frees itself of the walls and prepares itself for the climb up to the pass. On the final approach to the top of the pass the path swings right to assume a northeasterly direction.

❹ Scandale Pass NY388096
The top of the pass is a wild place, hemmed between the scabby slopes of Red Screes (right) and Little Hart Crag (left).

D▶ From the pass, climb north-northwest on the east side of a dry-stone wall. The path veers left along the north side of Scandale Tarn, a lonely place with views back to Windermere and Morecambe Bay.

You could stay on this path as it continues to High Beckstones (Bakestones), the cairn on the horizon. But it's better to leave it before the tarn and climb north across pathless slopes to Black Brow on the Little Hart Crag ridge; it's just west of the main summit. If you are in any doubt, a nearby fence goes in the same direction. The reason for leaving the comfort of the path will now be evident. From any of the rocky perches on

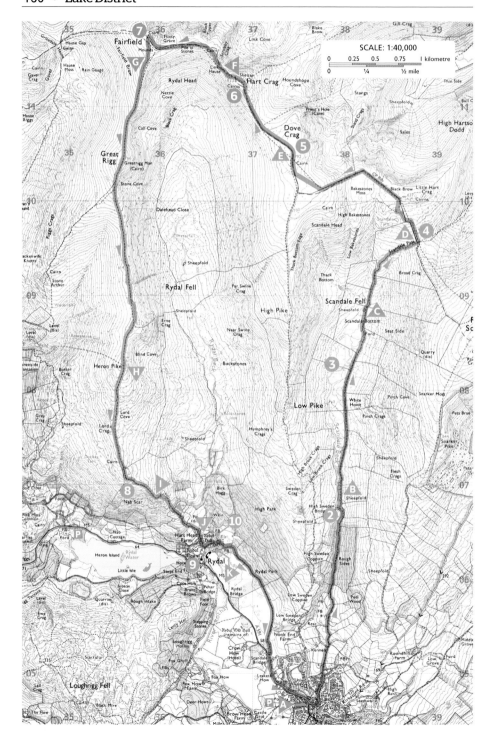

SCALE: 1:40,000

0   0.25   0.5   0.75   1 kilometre

0   ¼   ½ mile

Dove Crag from the slopes of Hart Crag

Black Brow you can look over bold cliffs into the deep scoop of Hogger Gill to Brotherswater and Hartsop.

The route now climbs northwest by the fence. Across Bakestones/Beckstones Moss it veers half left and the climb gets steeper. With height gain come new views across the cliffs of Dove Crag to Helvellyn's Striding Edge. The path meets the main Dove Crag ridge south of the summit. Turn right here and follow the side path by the ridge wall.

5 Dove Crag NY374105
Dove Crag's summit has got a rocky platform with a little cairn but its plateau is expansive and you need to go to the edges for the best views.

E The path continues by the wall, descending rocky slopes to a col overlooking a shady corrie, Hunsett Cove (Houndshope Cove on OS maps), and the lower reaches of Dovedale. Now the path clambers up the rocks to reach the summit of Hart Crag.

6 Hart Crag NY368113
Hart Crag is a more spectacular place than Dove Crag. Its summit is smaller, rockier and has two cairns. It overlooks three fine valleys, those of Dovedale, Deepdale and Rydal Beck. But Hart Crag too has its peers, for the great mass of Fairfield lies to the west.

F Descend the rocky slopes to Link Hause, a narrow saddle overlooking the dark craggy confines of Link Cove, then start the climb across the stony eastern arm of Fairfield. The cairned path rounds Rydal Head, with views down the long barren valley of Rydal Beck, to reach Fairfield summit.

7 Fairfield NY358117

The high point of the whole route, Fairfield's huge domed plateau dominates the head of Grisedale, Deepdale, the Rydal valley and Tongue Gill. Its stony top is scattered with cairns and wind shelters.

The most spectacular view is to the north, where the cliffs and corries of Dollywaggon and Nethermost Pikes lead the eye to Helvellyn and Striding Edge. Down steep slopes to the right is a fine little pyramid of rock and scree, Cofa Pike, and behind that the dome of St Sunday Crag. The familiar outlines of the Scafells, the Langdales, Pillar and Great Gable are stretched across the western horizon, while to the south the return route to Ambleside is etched on the long, grassy spine of Great Rigg and Heron Pike.

G Fairfield summit is gently rounded, and a tricky place in mist. Use a compass if necessary to head south and find the top of the spur leading down towards Great Rigg. Once on the spur, the path is clear. The ridgeline levels, then climbs slightly to the high but undistinguished top of Great Rigg. On the following descent, be careful not to be enticed onto a path on the right towards Stone Arthur and Grasmere – keep on the main path, with steep drops immediately to your left.

Ridge north of Heron Pike

H Heron Pike comes next; this is easy ridgewalking with airy views across Grasmere and Easedale. The summit has a small outcrop of rock with a band of quartzite in it. At Nab Scar there's a ladder stile over a dry-stone wall, the first one encountered for some time. The path veers left soon after and begins the steep descent.

8 The Thirlmere Aqueduct NY356068

The Thirlmere Aqueduct runs under Nab Scar, and there's a small stone marker just off the path. The aqueduct was built in 1906 to carry water from Thirlmere to the Manchester area.

I The path descends in zigzags, confined by erosion control fences. In the lower reaches it has been heavily engineered. It joins a lane just above Rydal Mount.

9 Rydal Mount NY364065

Rydal Mount was home to William Wordsworth from 1813 until his death in 1850. He moved here from the Rectory at Grasmere following the tragic deaths of two of his children. The house contains family portraits, some of the poet's personal possessions, and first editions of some of his works.

The gardens were designed by Wordsworth himself – he wrote many of his later poems on the terrace here. While here and at the age of 73, Wordsworth was made Poet Laureate, in succession to his friend, Robert Southey. By this time his most important works were long past, and he had become a pillar of society – Distributor of Stamps for Westmorland. Nearby, Dora's Field was a gift from Wordsworth to his daughter. The daffodils he planted still bloom in spring. The house is open daily from March to October and on most days in November, December and February.

Descending the lane past Rydal Mount, turn left on the signposted track, the upper of two entrances to Rydal Hall.

⑩ Rydal Hall NY366064

Rydal Hall was built in the seventeenth century, with eighteenth-century additions, and was home to the Le Fleming family for 300 years. In 1909 they commissioned the famous landscape gardener, Thomas Mawson, to design the beautiful formal gardens around the hall. The waterfalls in the beck that flows through the estate have been painted by many celebrated artists. A pencil sketch by John Constable is kept at Abbott Hall in Kendal. In 1963 the Diocese of Carlisle bought the hall as a Christian retreat. There's also a conference centre, a tea shop, an outdoor youth centre, and a camp site.

The waymarked route passes the tea shop to the left of the main hall, which is not open to the public. Beyond all the buildings, follow the fenced estate road as it loops back through a parkland set with some fine horse chestnut trees. Beyond impressive ornamental boundary gates the track meets the main Ambleside road. Turn left along the road, following it past the police station and back to the car park.

Helvellyn from Fairfield summit

Wansfell Pike & Troutbeck

START/FINISH:
Main car park at Ambleside
(NY376047)

DISTANCE/ASCENT:
6 miles (9.5km) / 1,700ft
(525m)

APPROXIMATE TIME:
3 hours

HIGHEST POINT:
Wansfell Pike summit
1,588ft (484m)

MAP:
OS Explorer OL7;
OS Landranger 90;
Harveys Lakeland Central and
Lakeland East

REFRESHMENTS:
Mortal Man (pub), Troutbeck;
teas at Troutbeck Post Office

ADVICE:
An easy route with only
one moderate climb to
Wansfell Pike

This short route to Ambleside's mountain starts, fittingly, at Ambleside, takes in the Stock Ghyll Force waterfalls, then the Pike itself. The climb is a steady one, but once it is over, this is an easy walk that ambles down to secluded Troutbeck before returning to Ambleside, with fine views of Windermere, and maybe the sun setting over the Langdale Pikes.

❶ Ambleside NY376043
Ambleside has a history dating back to the Romans, who had their fort, Galava, on the northern shores of Windermere. However, this bustling town is largely Victorian, and grew from the profits of tourism. In those early days visitors would arrive at Windermere by railway, to take a steamer trip along the lake to Waterhead before continuing by carriage on the turnpike road into Ambleside itself.

Ⓐ After turning right out of the car park, follow the bustling main road past Bridge House and bear left through the centre of Ambleside. Turn left along the short alley between Barclays Bank and the Market Hall, then left again along Stock Ghyll Lane. The lane bends right to climb parallel to the deep, wooded gill. A footpath on the left lets you into Stock Ghyll Park wood.

❷ Stock Ghyll Park Wood NY385048
This path was very popular with Victorians, who would have paid threepence at a turnstile to see the falls. The force of the water itself was used to power the water wheels of several fulling mills. The wheel of the lowest one in the centre of Ambleside has been preserved.

Ⓑ Take the left fork down steps to a footbridge over the gill before climbing above the north bank through beech, oak, elm and hazel trees to view Stock Ghyll Force. Here two cascades join forces, plunging into a deep and turbulent pool.

Cross the bridge above the falls then turn right back down the valley. At the next fork, take the left path, which veers away from the gill to bring you to a wrought iron Victorian turnstile. Turn left up the lane towards Grove Farm but leave the lane for a path up steps on the right, signposted

'Troutbeck via Wansfell'. Over the stile the route climbs up high pastures with a small stream on the left. The gradients become steeper on the upper flanks of the fell but the path is well built all the way. It crosses the stream. A dry-stone wall comes in from the left. Go through a gap in it, then over a ladder stile in a wall to get to the summit.

3 Wansfell Pike NY394042

The top is a superb place to be, with interesting views in all directions. You can look down the entire length of Windermere and its lush green surroundings. Looking back the way you came, you can see Ambleside, with the church steeple prominent, backed up by knobbly Loughrigg, the Coniston Fells and the jagged outlines of the Langdale Pikes. To the east, the bare stony fellsides of Froswick, Ill Bell and Yoke rear up from the fields of the Troutbeck valley.

 The well built path off Wansfell Pike descends eastwards across drab marshy slopes before going through a gate in a wall. Continue for a short way east to meet an enclosed track, Nanny Lane. Turn right along this rough track, which winds down into Troutbeck village at Lane Foot Farm.

4 Troutbeck NY410031

The Mortal Man inn was built in 1689, but was substantially rebuilt and enlarged late in the nineteenth century. Its sign reads:

'Oh Mortal Man Who Lives By Bread, What Is It That Makes Thy Nose So Red. Thou Silly Fool That Looks So Pale, Tis By Drinking Sally Birkett's Ale'.

Stock Ghyll Force

Ambleside from the slopes of Wansfell Pike

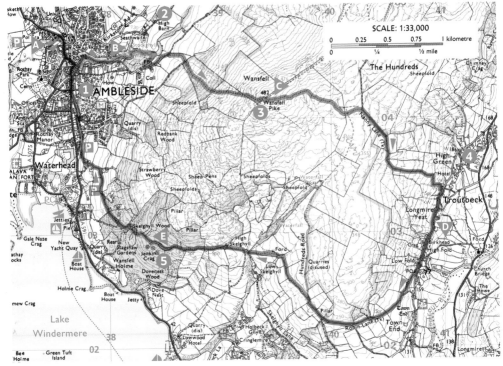

This is a copy of the original inn sign, which was painted by Julius Caesar Ibbotson, who lived here between 1802 and 1805.

Buildings in Troutbeck date back to the sixteenth century. Many still have mullioned windows and large cylindrical chimneys. The Spinnery, opposite the post office, has a fine

Robin Lane, Troutbeck

example of a spinning gallery. Townend, built as a yeoman farmer's house in 1626 by George Browne, was the family home until 1943 when it was bought by the National Trust. It is open to the public between April and October and illustrates the life of Lakeland's wealthy farmers in past centuries.

View across Windermere from Jenkin Crag

▶ Follow the road south through the village, past St Margaret's Well and two more dedicated to Saints James and John to the post office, then take a right fork along the tarmac track named Robin Lane and signposted as a bridleway. It climbs above Town End, shaded by sycamore, holly and ash trees.

Ignore the two tracks on the left, which descend south to Holbeck Lane. Instead, stay with the main track, which rounds the flanks of Wansfell, eventually to assume a course northwest. The lane changes its name to Hundreds Road and veers north and is no longer any use to this route. A gate on the left marks the start of a path, signposted to Skelghyll and Ambleside. It descends across a field, through another gate, then fords a stream.

By the waterside here you may see lesser spearworts, with their yellow, buttercup-like flowers, the purple-blue of Devil's-bit scabious, and the small white flowers of the grass of Parnassus.

A fence on the right guides the path to a surfaced lane leading to High Skelghyll Farm. Behind the farm are the pale outcrops of Coniston Limestone.

Through the farmyard a rough track heads west into Skelghyll Wood, owned by the National Trust. A sign on the left points out the detour to Jenkin Crag. The detour passes through a gap in a dry-stone wall to reach one of Lakeland's most popular viewpoints.

⑤ Jenkin Crag NY385028

Huge fragmented outcrops from the Borrowdale Volcanic Group look out over the tops of the trees, across Windermere and the green fields and wood of Skelwith to the peaks of the Coniston Fells and the Langdale Pikes.

▶ Retrace your steps to the main track and follow it left through the wood. The track divides – the left branch is a steeper short-cut. The paths rejoin to cross a stone bridge over Stencher Beck, where waterside rocks are colonised by mosses, liverworts and ferns. Beyond the beck the path continues gently downhill and out of the wood to a tarmac lane. This descends further to the Old Lake Road. For the best return route through Ambleside, turn left past the Ambleside and Langdale Mountain Rescue Centre, then right, following the main Lake Road past the garden centre.

Windermere from High Skelghyll

Place Fell

Place Fell may belong to Patterdale but it's better to sneak up on it, following the back roads on the east side of Ullswater to Sandwick. Take your time and take in the ever-changing views of craggy fellsides, waterfalls and that long languishing lake, which reaches out to touch the lowlands of Penrith.

1 Sandwick NY423197
At Sandwick, the waters of Boredale and Howe Grain becks join forces to squeeze past Hallin and Sleet Fells and empty into Ullswater. A few cottages cluster by the fellsides at the end of a small winding lane. There is room for a few cars on the grassy verges past Doegreen Farm, but take care not to block local traffic.

A Walk along the lane towards Sandwick. Turn left at a signpost marked 'Bridlepath to Patterdale' beside a tall dry-stone wall before climbing left on a narrow grassy track through dense bracken on the steep slopes of Sleet Fell, passing a metal seat. Turn right at a crossroads of paths, raking across the fell's western slopes, crossing streams.

2 Scalehow Force NY414190
Scalehow Beck scurries down the hillside below you on the right, then tumbles below the crags of High Knott in a spectacular waterfall that disappears into the trees. You'll see it better on the return leg of the walk.

Martindale and Hallin Fell, seen from the start of the walk at Sandwick

START/FINISH:
Sandwick on the east side of Ullswater (NY423194). A good alternative is to park in Glenridding and get the ferry across Ullswater to Howtown (in the summer), then use the linking lakeside path to Sandwick (see Walk 28)

DISTANCE/ASCENT:
7½ miles (12km) / 2,000ft (600m)

APPROXIMATE TIME:
5 hours

HIGHEST POINT:
Place Fell summit 2,156ft (657m)

MAP:
OS Explorer OL5;
OS Landranger 90;
Harveys Lakeland Eastern

REFRESHMENTS:
The Howtown Hotel (Easter-November) Side Farm (off route)

ADVICE:
The route beneath Mortar Crag to the Knight could be confusing in mist. In such conditions it would be better to follow the more defined path climbing southwest to Place Fell's summit

B Keep to the path which climbs above and to the left of High Knott. It makes good progress round the rocks on the flank of High Dodd and passes a ruined stone building before making the grassy ridge on Low Moss. Here the main High Street ridges come into view across Martindale. Turn right on a well-worn path past some ruined stone sheepfolds.

As the ground steepens beyond the sheepfold take the right fork rather than the busier direct path to Place Fell. The sunken grassy path rounds Place Fell's western slopes, passing above Mortar Crag. Here you can see Ullswater stretching to the northeastern horizon where the hills merge with the lowland fields of Penrith.

Brotherswater from Place Fell

The little-used path degenerates into a sheep-track. Ignore the large beacon-like cairn topping the crags on the left, and instead stick with the track that leads towards a bold rocky outcrop known as The Knight. Cross the narrow stream at its foot, then turn uphill, to right of the stream, across tussocky ground to a nick between Place Fell's high crags. The summit trig juts out into the skyline but disappears as the path tucks in beneath the crags. You should emerge on the ridge by a large but shallow pool where a prominent path climbs those last rocks guarding the summit.

③ Place Fell NY405169
The stone-built trig point rests on an outcrop of gritty ribbed rock and gives new and wide views of Brotherswater, which usually glimmers like a precious stone beneath Red Screes and Caudale Moor. The Helvellyn range yawns across the western horizon, while its mirror image, the High Street range, does the same thing to the east. Each is intricately set with corries and crag.

C▸ Descend southwards past the cairn on Round How where the path drops steeply down to Boredale Hause. At Chapel in the Hause, turn right on the bridleway which descends towards Patterdale and Ullswater. Two paths run side by side, not 50yds (45m) apart: yours will be the upper one which hugs craggy slopes laced with bracken, heather and hawthorn.

D▸ The two paths join and descend towards Place Fell House. Just before the house a narrow path avoids that last descent and rakes across the hillside. It weaves past a quarry, an interesting cave by a cascading stream, and a small seat that gives pleasing views of the lake and the villages of Patterdale and Glenridding, which are dwarfed by the high fells of the Helvellyn range.

Looking north from Place Fell

The path climbs to a nick between Silver Crag and Birk Fell, then plummets past juniper bushes to Silver Bay, ever nearer to the lakeshores. In winter this stretch is sunless and can become treacherously icy.

A good stony path undulates through the shoreline woodlands and rounds Birk Fell before skirting Scalehow Woods. From hereabouts Scalehow Force looks even better than it did earlier in the day. Being higher than the path it drops from the sky down its mossy rocks.

④ Scalehow Beck NY415192

The path nears Scalehow Beck, where you may see that skittish bird, the dipper. This small black bird with a white collar gets its name from its habit of dipping up and down while standing on a waterside boulder. To catch its usual prey of larval insects, the dipper can swim beneath the fast-flowing water, and even walk along the bottom, using half spread wings to hold itself down.

The path follows a tall dry-stone wall, and crosses Scalehow Beck on a wooden footbridge to lead back to the road at Sandwick.

Ullswater

Apart from the Haweswater Reservoir, every one of Lakeland's lakes can reasonably claim to be the loveliest of them all. But of the lakeside paths the loveliest, as well as the longest, is along the eastern shore of Ullswater. It leads from the edge of the Lake District to the very foot of Helvellyn by way of woods, rocks and little streams. Lunch time is at the Howtown Hotel; teatime is at Glenridding; and the return is by lake steamer.

A Follow signposts for Howtown, to turn right beside the church. Keep ahead across the road above, as a brown tourist information sign indicates Hill Croft Camp Site. The tarred lane passes the entrance to the site. It climbs to a gate onto open moorland, with a rough track continuing beyond. After 1 mile (1.5km) is a four-way signpost and a large cairn. Howtown is indicated to the right. From the signpost the way continues south as a sketchy track to a stone circle called the Cockpit.

❶ The Cockpit Stone Circle NY483222

Although at this point we have views of craggy country ahead, we are standing outside the true Lake District on the younger limestone of the surrounding country. Just off the line of our route, at NY487234 on Heughscar Hill, is a small area of limestone pavement. The stones of the Cockpit are limestone, and the mud of the sketchy track is limestone mud and extra sticky. The short section between the signpost and

START:
Pooley Bridge (NY471244)

FINISH:
Glenridding pier (NY390169) with return by lake steamer to Pooley Bridge

DISTANCE/ASCENT:
12 miles (19.5km) / 1,800ft (550m)

APPROXIMATE TIME:
7½ hours

HIGHEST POINT:
Cockpit Stone Circle 1,050ft (320m)

MAP:
OS Explorer OL5;
OS Landranger 90;
Harveys Lakeland East and Lakeland Central

REFRESHMENTS:
Howtown Hotel; Patterdale; Glenridding. Pooley Bridge too has inns and cafés, many of which serve chilled desserts even without the aid of stored ice from Lanty Tarn

ADVICE:
An initial boat trip to Howtown will halve the walk. Leave Pooley Bridge before 9.00am for the last boat back at 4.45pm (summer timetable), though there are later buses back. The energetic can divert at Sandwick onto Walk 27 (Place Fell) – allow an extra 1½ hours for that

Ullswater morning

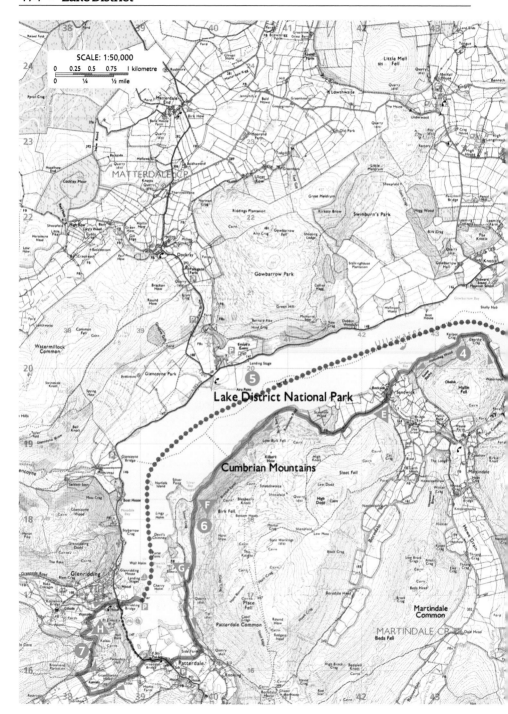

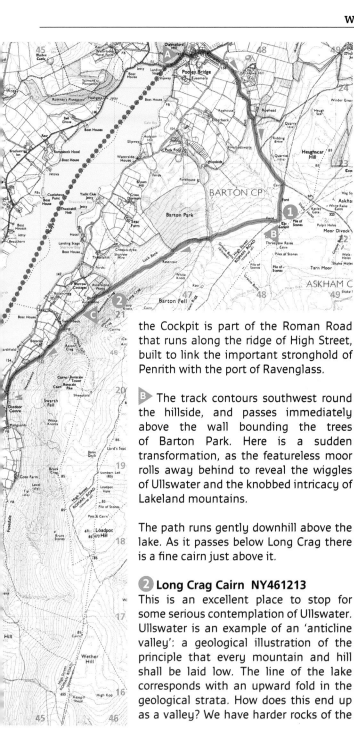

the Cockpit is part of the Roman Road that runs along the ridge of High Street, built to link the important stronghold of Penrith with the port of Ravenglass.

B The track contours southwest round the hillside, and passes immediately above the wall bounding the trees of Barton Park. Here is a sudden transformation, as the featureless moor rolls away behind to reveal the wiggles of Ullswater and the knobbed intricacy of Lakeland mountains.

The path runs gently downhill above the lake. As it passes below Long Crag there is a fine cairn just above it.

2 Long Crag Cairn NY461213

This is an excellent place to stop for some serious contemplation of Ullswater. Ullswater is an example of an 'anticline valley': a geological illustration of the principle that every mountain and hill shall be laid low. The line of the lake corresponds with an upward fold in the geological strata. How does this end up as a valley? We have harder rocks of the

Borrowdale Volcanic on top and softer Skiddaw Slates below. Erosion tends to take the tops off things. Once the top was off the long Ullswater fold, there was a line of softer rock exposed ready to be worn down into a valley.

C The narrow track remains just above the top field wall, passing above Auterstone Wood and crossing a footbridge below the impressive ravine of Swarthbeck Gill. After another ¾ mile (1.2km), the path passes immediately above a house; just after this, a small gate down right is marked 'No Cycles'.

Small steps lead down into a field with white-topped marker posts. At the road below, cross to Howtown Pier.

3 Howtown NY444198
Howtown has a hotel, and the Ullswater Steamer (now converted to diesel) can transfer you effortlessly to Glenridding if necessary, or take you back to Pooley Bridge.

D Continue along the lakeshore, and climb earth steps to the left of Waternook Farm. The path leads right, through the oaks of Hallinhag Wood. Feet slip on oak roots and eyes peer out between oak leaves to the first views of Helvellyn and the other large hills clustered around the head of the lake.

4 Kailpot Crag NY434204
In 1961 Manchester Corporation asked Parliament to let it dam the outflow of Ullswater and start using it as a reservoir. That the Bill was defeated was largely due to the efforts of Lord Birkett QC, a draper's son from Ulverston. Those who knew him considered that the effort he put into

the campaign cost him his life: he died a few hours after making the decisive speech in the House of Lords. Just at the beginning of Hallinhag Wood an inscription has been carved in his memory in the lakeside rock below the path. It can only be seen from the lake, and is placed where it will be obliterated if the level of the water should ever be artificially raised. An inconspicuous and formerly nameless fell on the other side of the lake has been named in his honour.

More recently, the limiting of power boats on the lake has led to an increase in nesting birds, including goosander and cormorant.

▶ At Sandwick, head left, up the road, for 110yds (100m), then continue on a grassy bridleway track on the right. Even better than Hallinhag is the stony up-and-down through the woods below Long Crag.

⑤ Aira Point NY404198
Ullswater's name may derive from a Saxon word for elbow, or it may come from a Norseman called Ulf or Ulfa. Ulf dragged his longboat inland to reach the lake, and built his settlement on the flat wooded ground of Aira Point immediately opposite. Lyulph's Tower, that stands there today, is a Victorian pile in romantic massive stone – very suitable for this particular landscape.

▶ At the end of the wood, at Silver Bay, the path divides. A broad, easy path runs forward at the same level: but even nicer is the one that climbs left from a sprawling cairn. This higher path is eroded at first, then climbs into the narrow col behind Silver Crag.

Glenridding from just below Lanty's Tarn at the very end of the walk, with mist over Ullswater

Ullswater Steamer approaches
Howtown

⑥ Silver Crag NY397180

In this little pass, juniper and grey rock form a combination that is typical of Lakeland, and as pleasing as a Japanese bonsai arrangement. Juniper scrub appears to the casual eye to be no more than a patch of gorse, but closer approach reveals an aromatic evergreen, with twisted reddish bark, and purple berries in late summer. Once noticed, you see juniper everywhere, and it is in fact the world's most widespread tree. It survives here on steep rocky slopes where sheep have been unable to nibble the young trees.

On the small island opposite, called House Holm (Norfolk Island on OS maps), naturalists were puzzled to discover in 1957 a colony of short-tailed voles. They must have arrived by walking across the ice, or by floating across on an ice floe.

Ⓖ Drop right on a descending path to rejoin the lower path, then pass along the top of Side Farm's camp site to Side Farm itself. A small shop selling sweets and ice cream is also a tea room and serves excellent home-made cakes from Easter to October. Turn right, down the farm's driveway, into Patterdale. (If you're too late for the ferry, there's a bus from Patterdale at 5.10pm.)

From here to Glenridding a footpath runs alongside the road, below trees. If time allows, it's better to climb to Glenridding past Lanty's Tarn. This route turns left at the end of Patterdale in a narrow tarred lane. After ⅔ mile (1km) the lane ends at a gate; without going through it, turn right across a bridge and take a small path ahead that goes straight up a field.

At the field top turn right through a gate, and after 22yds (20m) bear up left on a wide path to Lanty's Tarn. This is a small reservoir below trees.

⑦ Lanty's Tarn NY384163
The name Lanty is a corruption of Lancelot, after Lancelot Dobson who owned most of Grisedale. The tarn was enlarged for a surprising purpose – to supply ice for the Marshalls of Patterdale Hall. Ice was cut into blocks with two-handed saws. In normal use, the 'underdog' was the person at the lower end of such a saw, who had to work in an enclosed pit under a rain of sawdust. It was a traditional joke to persuade any young worker who had never taken part in 'Ice Day' to take the nasty end of the saw, standing under water in the frozen tarn. The ice was stored under 3ft (1m) of sawdust in the nearby icehouse until it was needed to provide chilled desserts throughout the summer.

As the path emerges from the trees at the head of the little tarn, there is a sudden and stunning view over the top of Glenridding and along the length of Ullswater. Out in that view, its ripples spreading across the evening water, slowly passes the last ferry to Pooley Bridge, sending ripples across the evening water. How are you going to get back to your car now?

🇭 A zigzag path drops into the edge of Glenridding, where a right turn along a track takes you to the main road through the village. The pier is on the right.

Ullswater Steamer at Glenridding Pier

Angle Tarn & High Street

START/FINISH:
Car park at Cow Bridge near Hartsop (NY403134)

DISTANCE/ASCENT:
10 miles (16km) / 2,400ft (730m)

APPROXIMATE TIME:
6½ hours

HIGHEST POINT:
High Street 2,717ft (828m)

MAP:
OS Explorer OL5;
OS Landranger 90;
Harveys Lakeland East

REFRESHMENTS:
Nearest are at Patterdale to the north, or the Brotherswater Inn and Kirkstone Pass Inn to the south

ADVICE:
The descent off Gray Crag is steep, and would be difficult in wintry conditions

The mountains of Lakeland get a little less rocky east of the Kirkstone Pass. They get a little lower too, but don't let that put you off, for the High Street range has most of what the Helvellyn range has, just in smaller quantities. For Striding Edge, read Long Stile; for Red Tarn, read Blea Tarn; for the Dodds read Loadpot Hill and Wether Hill. You can get up High Street without waiting for the crowds or some nervous walker to move aside from the crags; and there is a Roman road as well!

① Cow Bridge NY403134

Cow Bridge has a handy roadside car park that saves the narrow lanes of Hartsop from being invaded by walkers' cars. It is beautifully positioned by the banks of Goldrill Beck, a cool, crystal stream babbling in the shadows of Low Wood's hillside oaks.

Ⓐ From the car park at Cow Bridge, turn right down the main road, then left on the lane towards Hartsop. After a short way turn left again by the adventure centre on a narrow tarmac lane heading north. The lane becomes a stony track. Where it bends right towards some wooden chalets keep straight on along a wide walled track beneath the woods of Calf Close.

The track passes beneath the cascades of Angletarn Beck. Beyond Dubhow Farm leave the track for a path raking up

Walking along the shore of Angle Tarn with St Sunday Crag and Helvellyn on the skyline

the hillslopes to the right, high above Beckstones Farm. The path eventually veers right to cross Stonebarrow Gill, as paths from Patterdale join in from the left. It then climbs alongside the gill's slaty gorge to Boredale Hause.

2 Boredale Hause NY408157

At Boredale Hause, what looks like a run-down sheep enclosure is really the ruin of a mediaeval chapel that served the parishioners of both Martindale and Patterdale.

Harter Fell and High Street from Rampsgill Head

B▶ Beyond the old chapel and by a cairn, the path recrosses the beck to climb southwards and into a shallow ravine. On reaching the skyline it veers left on Stony Rigg with pleasing views over Dubhow Brow to Brotherswater.

As the little path turns left beyond Dubhow Beck, it splits into two. Either fork will do. The left one goes higher, beneath the rocks of Angletarn Pikes, and loses a bit of height as it nears the shores of Angle Tarn. The lower, narrower right fork gives excellent views of Brotherswater and the landscape leading up to the top of the Kirkstone Pass. Beyond Dubhow Brow it swings left towards Angle Tarn.

3 Angle Tarn NY417144

Angle Tarn hides behind its surrounding little green hills until the last moment. When you see it for the first time you wonder how something this big can hide for so long. The glaciers that carved out the valleys either side of the ridge also left the debris that traps the waters of the tarn. It's an attractive tarn too, with two small islands, some rock buttresses on the shoreline, scattered windblown birches, and a wide and wonderful western horizon encompassing the Fairfield and Helvellyn mountain groups.

If you arrive early enough in the morning or late enough in the evening you may see a herd of red deer drinking here. They come from the Martindale Deer Park down in the valley. More likely, you'll see some of the wild fell ponies.

C▶ The path rounds the tarn on its left-hand (east) side. Once past, it climbs southeast towards Satura Crag. The path divides on meeting a stone wall (NY422138). The one on the right is the right of way, but the one on the left through a gate is the superior course. In its early stages it gives marvellous views into Bannerdale, a deep valley surrounded by the pale crag-fringed slopes of Beda Fell and The Nab.

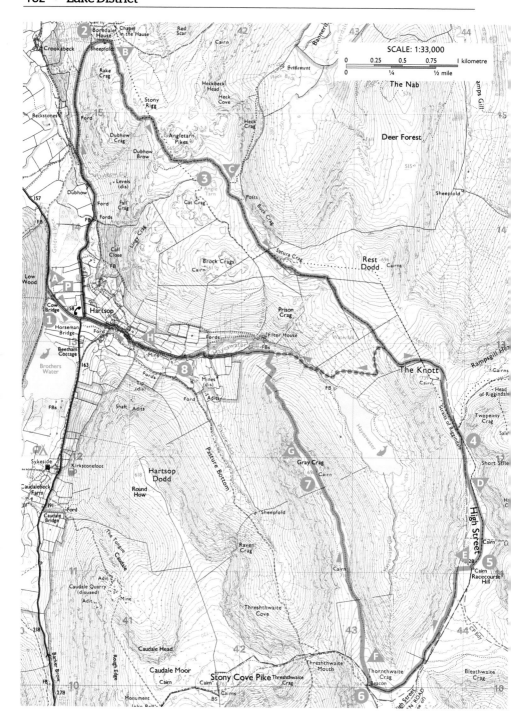

SCALE: 1:33,000

The Knott, seen across Hayeswater from Gray Crag

Follow the path as it climbs, keeping the wall, which later becomes a fence, to the right, and the dome of Rest Dodd straight ahead. By now Hayeswater has come into view, surrounded by the steep-sided Gray Crag and an equally steep-sided peak, The Knott.

The fence turns right at an intersection with a wall. Turn right on a path that gradually veers away from the fence to cross some marshy ground. The path crosses Sulphury Gill, then climbs left towards the Knott, going through a gap near a wall corner. The ground by now has become more bouldery. It's perfectly feasible to do a short detour to take in the summit of the Knott, but the path goes round to the left behind it. (In case of worsening weather, the path down to the right before the Knott is the last escape route back to Hartsop.)

The impressive cliffs of Rampsgill Head are now straight ahead, and you may want to make a detour towards them for the views down the length of Ramps Gill towards Martindale Common.

The path itself continues south by the ridge wall along the Straits of Riggindale. The narrowing saddle gives airy views both sides, down to Hayeswater (right) and into the hollow of Riggindale Beck (left). Here Kidsty Pike and the craggy spur of Long Stile frame a glimpse of Haweswater – it's all looking mountainous and spectacular now.

The High Street Roman road, which has been joined by the path from Kidsty Pike, comes in from the left and the course uphill to High Street (the mountain) is now wider and bolder.

Hayeswater from Thornthwaite Beacon, showing Gray Crag (left) and the Knott (right)

④ High Street Roman Road NY440121
Between AD80 and AD90 the Romans built their road along the course of an existing road, Brettestrete (the Britons' street), to link the forts at Galava, near Ambleside, and Brocavum, at Penrith. They built it on high ground as it was harder to be ambushed by the Celts up there, and there was none of the boggy woodland of the valleys to be cleared.

▶ In fact High Street (the road) doesn't actually make the summit of High Street (the mountain) for it takes a tamer line across its right shoulder. So, to get the mountain in, you have to follow the wall to the summit trig point.

⑤ High Street Summit NY441111
The summit itself is a bit disappointing: you have to go to its edges to get the best views, but the one over Blea Water and Riggindale Crags to the rocky Harter Fell is a good one.

High Street was once known as Racecourse Hill, a name dating back to the times when locals from the village of Mardale Green used to meet here for their annual festival. Events included wrestling, fox-hunting and horse racing. The 'racehorses' were also used to carry ale and provisions for the revelry. The last meeting was held in 1835.

▶ From the summit descend west to rejoin the Roman road, but you soon leave it on a path forking right to round the head of Hayeswater's valley and visit the huge stone-built cairn, Thornthwaite Beacon.

⑥ Thornthwaite Beacon NY431100
From the 13ft- (4m-) high stone-built beacon you can look down Troutbeck's deep valley towards Windermere. You can

see the line of the Roman road as it rakes down the bare western flanks of Froswick, Ill Bell and Yoke.

▶ Keeping the wall on your left, descend north from the beacon down a grassy rake towards Gray Crag. There's a short rise to the cairn (710m) on the southern end of the ridge. The path continues along the crest to the northern summit. Although lower than the cairn you've just visited, this one is considered the true top of Gray Crag, and has finer views to prove it.

⑦ Gray Crag NY427118
From the northern summit of Gray Crag, Raven Crag looks dark and imposing across the deep gouge of Pasture Beck. The Knott now looks altogether a better sort of hill than it did on the approach from Angle Tarn. Its precipitous scree slopes and an impressive scree gully plummet into Hayeswater Reservoir and you can see down Hayeswater Gill to Hartsop.

▶ Coming off Gray Crag can be tricky in mist. It's very steep, and though it is mostly grass there are some crags on both sides to be avoided. The path descends steeply down the nose of the fell, becoming rockier in the middle reaches. Where it levels out above some crags (NY423126) a grassy path goes right and then zigzags down to the foot of the crags where the way is to the left near a broken wall. The path now bears right down the steep grassy fellside to join the stony track from Hayeswater some 55yds (50m) below the filter house.

Turn left along the track, passing the old lead mine workings, which lie at the foot of Pasture Beck's U-shaped glacial valley.

Gray Crag seen from the lane down to Hartsop

⑧ Myer's Head Lead Mine NY415127
The short-lived lead mines were operated from 1867 to 1878, but were always hampered by flooding. At one time there was a 33ft- (10m-) water wheel, but little remains now. Conservation work is now being carried out and the Myer's Head Lead Mine is a scheduled Ancient Monument.

▶ The track comes down to the village of Hartsop, passing seventeenth-century stone-built cottages – a couple of which have spinning galleries.

The lane through the village passes the adventure centre met on the outward route before coming to the Ullswater road. Turn right along the road to get back to the car park.

START/FINISH:
Car park at Mardale Head
(NY469107). At quieter times,
can start/finish at **7** Kentmere
(NY456041)

DISTANCE/ASCENT:
13 miles (21km) / 3,800ft
(1,160m). From Kentmere start,
10 miles (16.5km) / 2,500ft
(750m)

APPROXIMATE TIME:
9 hours.
From Kentmere start, 7 hours

HIGHEST POINT:
Thornthwaite Beacon 2,572ft
(784m)

MAP:
OS Explorer OL5;
OS Landranger 96;
Harveys Lakeland Eastern

REFRESHMENTS:
Lunches, teas and evening
meals at Maggs Howe B&B,
Kentmere; Haweswater Hotel;
Crown and Mitre, Bampton
Grange

It's logical for most people to walk the Kentmere fells
from Kentmere. But the trouble with this is that on most
weekends Kentmere can get choked with cars it cannot
cope with – maybe it's better to do something a bit more
imaginative.

On this route from Mardale Head, not only do you get to
climb the rocky paths up Ill Bell, Froswick and Yoke, but you
also see one of its best tarns, Small Water.

1 Old Mardale NY469107

In the region of Haweswater's small wooded island, Wood
How, lie the remains of the old village of Mardale Green.
The village of 100 people consisted of a pub, the Dun Bull,
a church surrounded by yew trees, and some whitewashed
cottages. William Wordsworth likened the original lake to
a lesser Ullswater. It had natural beaches where primroses
fringed the banks. In his *Coast to Coast* book, Wainwright
reminisced about hedgerows sweet with flowers and wild
roses.

The village's founder was Hugh Holmes who hid in a cave in
Riggindale after fleeing from King John. In 1216 King John
died and Hugh Holmes married a local girl. The family were
referred to as the Kings of Mardale. The last in their long line
was Hugh Parker Holme who died in 1885.

Harter Fell seen from the path at the head of Haweswater

Yoke, Ill Bell and Froswick from near Gavel Crag

Yoke, Ill Bell and Froswick from near Gavel Crag

In 1860 Eliza Linton wrote in *Guide to the Lake Country*: 'The church is picturesque enough, but it's by no means a rustic cathedral; the Royal Hotel (the Dun Bull) is a wretched wayside public house, where you can get eggs and bacon and nothing else – except the company of a tipsy parson lying in bed with his gin bottle by his side; and the King of Mardale – the great man of the place, is nothing better than a yeoman for all that.'

In 1919 the Manchester Water Authority managed to get their plan for a new reservoir in Mardale through Parliament. A new village was to be built for the residents at Burnbanks, and a new road would be routed down the higher west side of the valley.

Work began on the 120ft- (37m-) concrete dam, which would raise the water level by 96ft (29m) and flood much of the upper valley. To give some idea of the scale of the project, the village was more than a mile south of the old lakeshore.

In 1935, the Bishop of Carlisle took the last religious service at the church. It was later demolished and its stones used to construct the reservoir's control tower. Last orders were called at the Old Dun Bull; the cobbler and shopkeepers closed their doors. Then, ever so slowly, the waters of the new lake rose until, in 1941, Mardale Green was lost forever.

After periods of drought quiet reminders of the past come to light when the water level drops to reveal crumbling foundations and dry-stone walls and a crazed mosaic of

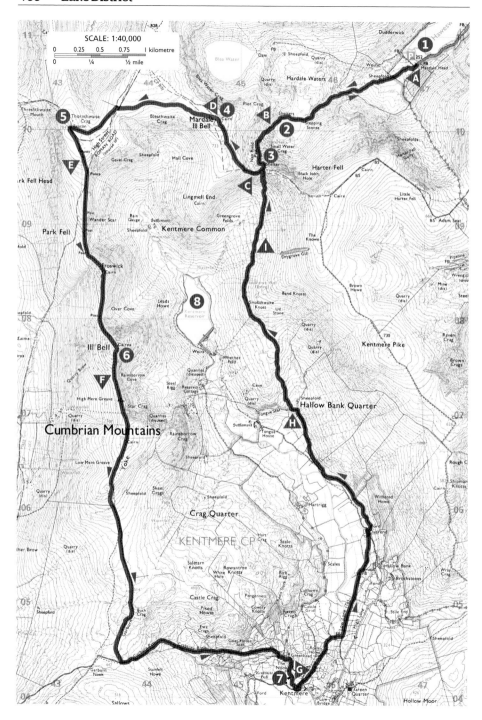

drying mud. Old photographs of village and valley can be seen in the Haweswater Hotel, halfway along the shores of the reservoir.

A From the car park follow the path across the footbridge over Gatescarth Beck. Ignore the signposted routes to Bampton (right) and Gatescarth Pass (to the left by the spruce plantation) and instead stay on the path going through the gate, then running parallel to Small Water Beck. This soon climbs beneath the dark crags of Harter Fell to more confined bouldery hillsides beside the beck. Soon it accompanies the stream to the outflow of Small Water, where it crosses the stream and rounds the tarn on its northern shores.

② Small Water NY455100
Small Water is one of the gems of eastern Lakeland, a splendid tarn set in a rocky corrie. It's a superb place for a picnic, though you reach it a bit early in the day.

Buzzards and ravens scour the corries hereabouts, but you may be lucky enough to see the mighty golden eagle, which nests in Mardale. The eyrie, less than a mile away, is the last stronghold in England and there's a 24-hour watch to ensure its safety.

This magnificent dark brown bird with a golden-coloured head and neck has a large hooked beak, and wings with a span of up to 6½ft (2m) and sharp talons. Immature eagles have more white on their wings and tail.

At one time the eagle was a common sight in the mountainous areas of England, Scotland and Wales, but the increasing urbanisation of the areas, overzealous gamekeepers and egg collectors led to the birds' confinement to the Highlands of Scotland.

A bird protection act of 1954 made it illegal to kill these birds of prey, and the eagles' numbers grew. They spread first to the Solway peninsula. Then in 1959 one was spied soaring over Cumberland. Just over ten years later, a breeding pair nested in the Lake District, and after one unsuccessful year, a chick was successfully reared, here in Mardale.

B The path now winds and climbs among the crags of Mardale Ill Bell's eastern flanks to reach Nan Bield Pass, a narrow cleft between Mardale Ill Bell and Harter Fell.

❸ Nan Bield Pass NY452096

A stone enclosure acts as a wind shelter at the pass, and it's often needed in this wild and inhospitable place.

You've been travelling on one of the ancient traders' routes and the dramatic setting can take you back to the time when smugglers brought in their bounties, perhaps booze and tobacco that had been smuggled across the seas to Ravenglass.

Back towards Mardale, the tear-shaped Small Water and its rocky basin look their best, and lead the eye to the headwaters of Haweswater. But new landscapes appear ahead as you look into Kentmere. Ill Bell boasts its precipitous flanks of rock and scree, which plummet to the scruffy shores of the Kentmere Reservoir.

▶ **C** We're not ready for Kentmere yet, for there are mountains to climb. First it's Mardale Ill Bell, not to be confused with the Kentmere Ill Bell. The path to the west climbs the craggy slopes, swinging first left, then right. Take the right fork halfway up the slope to gain the summit.

❹ Mardale Ill Bell NY447102

From Mardale Ill Bell's summit, a detour to the northern edge reveals another fine tarn, the larger Blea Tarn, which is captured by the rocky arms of this peak, the cliffs of High Street and the knife-edge spur, Long Stile.

▶ **D** From the shallow col west of the summit leave the well-defined path that heads for High Street and trend left to locate a narrower path at the Kentmere edge of the ridge. Do not bend further left round the top of the gully, but carry straight on (west) to meet and cross the Roman road, High Street, at NY436102. The path then rounds the head of Hayeswater Gill to the huge stone beacon on Thornthwaite Crag.

⑤ Thornthwaite Beacon NY431101
From the beacon you can look down the length of Troutbeck's deep valley towards Windermere. You can see the line of the Roman road as it rakes down the featureless western flanks of Froswick, Ill Bell and Yoke.

E▶ The continuing route descends Thornthwaite Crag's narrow, grassy south ridge. You can see from here that Froswick, the next fell, is almost a replica of the one after it, Ill Bell. The climb to Froswick's rocky top is short but steep. It's a case of deja vu on the little path up Ill Bell, which clambers up the steep rock slopes to the summit.

⑥ Ill Bell NY436077
Everything on Ill Bell, however, is just that bit better than on its kid brother, Froswick. Ill Bell's pyramid shape is that little bit more symmetrical, that little bit loftier; the fascinating crags that shade a small corrie, Over Cove, are that little bit more fascinating than Froswick's Wander Scar; and the summit, with three cairns and a good rock platform to sit on, is that bit better and more mountain-like.

F▶ The next peak, Yoke, is a little different. It has some fine rocks, in the Star and Rainsborrow Crags, and it has a good angular outline. But otherwise Yoke is little more than a grassy dome; once you're on it, it feels like the Pennines. With this in mind you can choose the path on the right which rounds its western shoulder, or, if you like peak-bagging, the one that goes over the top. The latter gives better views of Rainsborrow Cove across Kentmere Reservoir to Harter Fell. The two routes meet again south of the summit, and roughly follow the ridge wall to Garburn Pass.

Descending to Haweswater from Nan Bield

Here you meet the old drove road, a stony track linking Troutbeck and Kentmere. Turn left along it, descending beneath rugged hillslopes in the shadow of Buck Crag and Ewe Crags. The cottages of Kentmere village are scattered below amid flat, green fields of the valley floor.

The track meets a tarmac lane on the outskirts of the village by The Nook (farm). Turn right at the T-junction a short way on and follow the lane through the village to St Cuthbert's church.

7 Kentmere NY456041

Sixteenth-century Kentmere Hall, seen to the right, was built onto a fourteenth-century peel tower. It was home to 'the Apostle of the North', Bernard Gilpin, who became Archdeacon of Durham. In 1558 he was arrested for his criticism of the Roman Catholic Church and would have been burnt at the stake. However, on his way to trial in London, Gilpin broke his leg. During his convalescence Queen Mary died and was replaced by Protestant Queen Elizabeth I.

St Cuthbert's Church has sixteenth-century roof beams and a bronze memorial to Gilpin. On his death St Cuthbert's body was rested overnight in the church on its way to Durham.

G Follow the walled track from the east side of the church. It heads north out of the village. After 1/3 mile (500m) at NY460046 beyond Rook Howe Farm, the valley can be seen ahead and the track descends and veers right towards the River Kent. It should be abandoned for a path on the right, which begins through a squeeze stile in the wall and crosses the river by a footbridge. On the other side it climbs eastwards to another walled track known as Low Lane. Turn left along the lane to Overend, which lies at the end of a tarmac road from the village.

Beyond Overend Farm, take the higher more easterly bridleway heading northwest through fields beneath the craggy wooded slopes of Withered Howe.

H Further north, beneath the spur of Tongue Scar the path turns to the left through a gate in the dry-stone wall and over a shallow stream. It then tackles Tongue Scar, a rocky spur separating Kentmere from Ullstone Gill's ravine.

8 Kentmere Reservoir NY445080

The Kentmere Reservoir soon comes into view beneath the steep craggy ramparts of Ill Bell and Yoke. It is an impressive scene slightly marred by the quarries close to the dam.

I Ahead now is Mardale Ill Bell. It sends out a grassy spur, Lingmell End, which plunges to the reservoir shores. The path keeps to the east of the spur and zigzags up grassy slopes, which become more rocky as height is gained. Soon we are back at the high pass, Nan Bield. If you started at Kentmere, continue at **C** above. Otherwise it's downhill all the way. The route retraces this morning's steps past Small Water back to Mardale Head.

Kentmere from Mardale Ill Bell, showing Gavel Crag with Yoke, Ill Bell and Froswick behind